Creative Wri

Related titles from Palgrave Macmillan

Robert Graham, Helen Newall, Heather Leach, John Singleton (eds) *The Road to Somewhere: A Creative Writing Companion*
John Singleton and Mary Luckhurst (eds) *The Creative Writing Handbook*, 2nd edition
John Singleton, *The Creative Writing Workbook*

Creative Writing

A Practical Guide

Third Edition

Julia Casterton

palgrave
macmillan

First edition 1986
Second edition 1998
Third edition published 2005 by
PALGRAVE MACMILLAN

Palgrave Macmillan in the UK is an imprint of Macmillan Publishers Limited, registered in England, company number 785998, of Houndmills, Basingstoke, Hampshire RG21 6XS.

Palgrave Macmillan in the US is a division of St Martin's Press LLC, 175 Fifth Avenue, New York, NY 10010.

Palgrave Macmillan is the global academic imprint of the above companies and has companies and representatives throughout the world.

Palgrave® and Macmillan® are registered trademarks in the United States, the United Kingdom, Europe and other countries.

ISBN 978–1–4039–4541–9   hardback
ISBN 978–1–4039–4263–0   paperback

This book is printed on paper suitable for recycling and made from fully managed and sustained forest sources. Logging, pulping and manufacturing processes are expected to conform to the environmental regulations of the country of origin.

A catalogue record for this book is available from the British Library.

A catalog record for this book is available from the Library of Congress.

Printed and bound in Great Britain by the
MPG Books Group, Bodmin and King's Lynn

Contents

Preface to Third Edition   vi

Preface to First Edition   viii

Acknowledgements   ix

1   Why Write?   1

2   The Space we Inhabit   14

3   Bringing your Descriptions to Life   26

4   Making your Characters Speak   36

5   Making a Short Story   48

6   Speaking in Different Tongues, Different Tones   56

7   Hold the Tension, Hold the Energy   66

8   Myth and Making a Narrative   76

9   Developing your Narrative   90

10 Writing Poetry   97

11 Preparing your Poems for Performance and   123
    Publication

12 Love Writing   141

13 Doing your Research   151

14 Writing for yourself Alone   161

15 Reaching an Audience   174

Further Reading – Some Useful Websites and Addresses   181

Index   185

Preface to Third Edition

When *Creative Writing – A Practical Guide* was first published in 1986, it was a little book of no more than a hundred pages. That was because I was young in my writing life, and didn't yet know many of the questions I and my fellow writers would have to face. For the second edition, having begun to fathom just how great the influence of writing can be on a person's life, I added a chapter called 'Writing for yourself Alone', as well as new chapters on poetry and writing about love.

For this new edition I listened as carefully as I could to the needs of my writing students, and I also asked myself 'What would have been most useful for me to read once I'd committed myself to being a writer?' This is why there's a new chapter on poetry, on taking poems through to performance and publication; on making a narrative out of myth, our most ancient stories; and also a chapter on some of the many ways writers do their research. New writers often ask 'How is it done?', thinking that there might be a key to laying the groundwork for a novel or a script. This chapter describes how different writers each find their own key, and supplies guidelines to help you to discover your own.

About the author

Julia Casterton teaches creative writing at the City Literary Institute in central London, and is external examiner for the MA in creative writing at Nottingham Trent University. She has worked as an editor for *Ambit* arts magazine, and judged several poetry and short story competitions. Her publications include *Troublesome Cattle* and *Bottom's Dream from Smith Doorstop*, and her most recent books are *The Doves of Finisterre* which won the Jerwood Prize for the best first full collection of poems in 2004 and *Writing*

Poems – A Practical Guide. Her work has appeared in magazines and anthologies, and she has also participated in the translations for a book of Arab women's poetry.

Julia Casterton lives in London with her husband and has two daughters.

Preface to First Edition

I have written this book for people who want to write, who know there is a writer inside them, but who find the leap of taking themselves seriously, and so beginning to write every day, an all but impossible one to take. Equally, it is for those who have written but are now silent. If you are a writer (and if you are there is a kind of death in not writing) you have to make many new beginnings – because of all the things in your life that can make you, for a time, lose your tongue. I hope this book will encourage those who have been silenced to hear again their own writer's voice: to take the risk of beginning again.

Acknowledgements

I want to thank Maria McKay, Antoinette Vass, Nigel Young and Rick Stanwood, who helped me with different parts of my life, from child-care to companionship, while I wrote this book, and Tina Betts, who discussed the work of literary agents with me.

I also want to thank all the writers and artists who have generously shared with me the part that writing has played in their lives: George Parfitt, Tim May, Hilary Mellon, Victor Magor, Wendy Kettle, Barbara Krzyworzeka, Joyce Goldstein, Maureen Li, Janet Campbell, Chris Hardy, Pearl Bean and Luise Casson.

Emily Lezzeri and Kate Pemberton helped me prepare the type-script of the second edition. Chris Nawrat went the last mile with me in the final proof-reading and indexing. Any errors that persist are entirely his own.

The author and publishers wish to thank the following for permission to use copyright material:

Carcanet Press Ltd and New Directions Publishing Corp for William Carlos Williams, 'To a Solitary Disciple' from *Collected Poems 1909– 1939 Volume 1* by William Carlos Williams. Copyright © 1938 by New Directions Publishing Corp; Curtis Brown, London, on behalf of the author for material from Grace Nichols, 'Omen' from *I is a long mem-oried woman* by Grace Nichols. Copyright © Grace Nichols 1983; Faber and Faber Ltd for extracts from T. S. Eliot's 'East Coker' from *Four Quartets* and 'The Love Song of Alfred Prufrock' from *Collected Poems 1909–1962* by T. S. Eliot; and with Farrar, Strauss and Giroux LLC for Seamus Heaney, 'St Kevin and the Blackbird' from *The Spirit Level* by Seamus Heaney. Copyright © 1996 Seamus Heaney; HarperCollins Publishers Ltd for dictionary entry 'irony' from *Collins English Dictionary*. Copyright © HarperCollins Publishers Ltd; Harvard University Press and the Trustees of Amherst College for Emily Dickinson, 'After great pain, a formal feeling comes' from *The Poems of Emily Dickinson*, ed. Thomas H. Johnson. Copyright © 1951,

1955, 1979 by the President and Fellows of Harvard College; Larmore Literary Agency on behalf of the author for Margaret Atwood, 'Spelling' from *True Stories* by Margaret Atwood, first published in Canada by Oxford University Press and in the United States by Simon and Schuster. Copyright © 1981 by Margaret Atwood; W. W. Norton & Company, Inc and the author for extracts from Adrienne Rich, 'Sibling Mysteries' from *The Dream of Common Language: Poems 1974–1977* by Adrienne Rich. Copyright © 1978 by W. W. Norton & Company, Inc.; Adrienne Rich, 'Readings of History' from *Collected Early Poems: 1950–1970* by Adrienne Rich. Copyright © 1993, 1967, 1963 by Adrienne Rich; Adrienne Rich, 'In the Wake of Home' from *Your Native Land, Your Life: Poems* by Adrienne Rich. Copyright © 1986 by Adrienne Rich; and Adrienne Rich, 'Coast to Coast' from *A Wild Patience Has Taken Me This Far: Poems 1978–1981* by Adrienne Rich. Copyright © 1981 by Adrienne Rich; 'Why should not old men be mad' is reprinted with the permission of Scribner, an imprint of Simon & Schuster Adult Publishing Group, from *The Collected Works of W.B. Yeats*, volume 1: *The Poems, Revised*, edited by Richard J. Finneran. Copyright © 1940 by Georgie Yeats, copyright renewed © 1968 by Bertha Georgia Yeats, Michael Butler Yeats and Anne Yeats. Due acknowledgement must be made of the permission of AP Watt Ltd on behalf of Michael B Yeats; Copyright © Benjamin Zephaniah, 'Bought and Sold', *Too Black Too Strong* (Bloodaxe Books, 2001); Chrissie Gittins, Celia de la Hey, John Ringrose and Peter Godfrey.

Every effort has been made to trace the copyright holders but if any have been inadvertently overlooked the publishers will be pleased to make the necessary arrangement at the first opportunity.

1 Why Write?

I often wonder why I write. I've spent hours talking to friends, writers and non-writers about it. For the first 25 years of my life I was convinced that everybody was either writing or wanted to write a novel. Finally a woman I worked with told me in no uncertain terms that *she* had no such desire, which threw me utterly. I'd assumed she was writing in secret, as I was – pursuing a universal dirty habit that demanded solitude and a quiet place – when instead she was watching TV or out at the pub with friends: being social. Writing isn't usually a social activity, except when you're working on exercises together in a writers' group – and even then you'll find that you do most of your writing alone, in whatever space and time you can carve out for yourself.

One thing seems clear: it isn't as natural as breathing. The myth of the 'natural' writer, who spins vast, architectural webs of exalted verse or prose is a treacherous lie which many writers have done their best to rub out, only to watch it appear again, healthy as ever, in literary columns, popular films about literary 'giants', even in the biographies of writers. No matter how much writers protest, non-writers seem to like the idea that writing is easy, not the arduous manual, emotional and intellectual labour writers know it to be. Simone de Beauvoir expressed great irritation when someone implied that anyone could have written *The Memoirs of a Dutiful Daughter*. If anyone could have written it, why was she the only one to have done so? Writers constantly have to deal with this prejudice, and it is well worth remembering this before discussing writing with casual acquaintances.

I think people write because they need to. Lawrence Durrell described it as a way of becoming more human. This process can take the form of fly-fishing with some people, Japanese boxing or embroidery with others. With writers it takes the form of writing. It takes time to understand this need, but I believe that the more we write, the more fully we grasp why it is we want to, have to. In *A Room of One's Own* Virginia Woolf argues that even though a person's gift for writing may be small, it is nevertheless death to hide it. The writer, for whatever reasons, is compelled to write. She or he may be able to suppress the compulsion for months or even years, believing perhaps that there are more worthwhile, less selfish ways to spend one's time. But who can tell the damage we do to our writing voices when we roughly silence them for long stretches?

There is a magic in words. We wade around in so many glossy pointless circulars, so many yards of dubious newsprint, that it is easy to forget this primary fact: it is words, and our ability to speak and write, which make us human. Words give us power over every other creature and thing in the natural world. Those who cannot write have less power than those who can: their acts of naming are restricted to those who will listen to them, those in the immediate locality. They cannot easily communicate with other societies or with those who are not yet born, as people can who know how to write. Bertolt Brecht advises people who are hungry to learn the alphabet. Knowledge of the skills of literacy is an important step towards taking control of one's own life.

Many societies, our own included, have imposed severe penalties on those who have aspired to the power that writing can give. Ruling groups have found that their interests are best safeguarded if they are supported by a workforce which cannot think for itself in the coherent way writing affords. The agents of the Spanish Inquisition burned books, as did the Nazis. Books can be dangerous because the reading and writing of them involves us in an exercise of intellectual freedom.

Imaginative writings, whether poetry, fiction or plays, create another place for the reader to inhabit, offer an alternative world which may challenge the real one. They are, in the most fundamental sense, magical: they weave spells, they conjure something out of nothing. William Shakespeare writes:

> The poet's eye, in a fine frenzy rolling,
> Doth glance from heaven to earth, from earth to heaven;
> And as imagination bodies forth
> The forms of things unknown, the poet's pen
> Turns them into shapes, and gives to airy nothing
> A local habitation and a name.
>
> *A Midsummer Night's Dream*, Act V, Scene ii

and Margaret Atwood, in a poem called 'Spelling', writes:

> My daughter plays on the floor
> with plastic letters,
> red, blue and hard yellow,
> learning how to spell,
> spelling,
> how to make spells.
>
> And I wonder how many women
> denied themselves daughters,
> closed themselves in rooms,
> drew the curtains
> so they could mainline words.
>
> A word after a word
> after a word is power.

Shakespeare and Atwood seem to have different attitudes towards this magic. Shakespeare's poet is in a frenzy, possessed by the spirit of artistic creation. No sooner has he imagined something than his pen transforms imagination into characters on the page. It all sounds spontaneous, unconscious and ... easy. Atwood's daughter, on the other hand, and the women poets she imagines are doing something different with words. The daughter is *playing* with letters and *learning* how to spell. The women are shutting themselves off, choosing the high that comes from writing instead of accepting their place as bearers and nurturers of children. They are in conflict with what is expected of them. They don't imagine they can have their cake and eat it too.

Women, men and writing

Women and men stand in a different relationship to language and women writers should remember this fact, both while they are writing and when they receive rejection slips from publishers. To begin with, young girls and women are frequently told that they talk too much, make facile use of words and chatter idly. Talking is something they do easily but not well, it is said. It is also said that girls are more verbally adept and can express complex concepts more readily than boys. I think it is the critical statements, rather than the words of praise, that are more often uttered in the hearing of girls. For a girl to take up her pen at all, then, is an act of great self-assertion. She is expressing herself against the popular wisdom concerning her sex.

Far fewer articles in magazines are written by women than men. Why is this? Did something terrible happen to those verbally adept young girls as they grew older? Did they lose the pleasure of saying what they wanted to say? Or are they grown up and still writing but to no avail? Does no one want to read their work? Are the subjects they write about simply not engaging to the editors of these magazines? How many of the editors are women? These are questions that women writers have to ask, questions we cannot escape from.

Things are changing though. In Britain, we now have three publishing houses committed to women's writing and at least two of the large publishing companies now carry a separate list for books of special interest to women. This is great news for the new generation of women writers, but for some it is already too late. They have lost heart, stashed away their manuscripts and told themselves they were never really writers anyway.

However, that isn't to say that male writers have it easy. Finding a publisher is hard for all writers and we know from the letters and diaries of writers as important as Gerard Manley Hopkins, Joseph Conrad and Hermann Melville how painful it is when the writing will not come. But I do believe that women experience another, relentless denial of their powers, which begins as soon as they can speak, if not before, and makes the act of writing for them primarily an act of rebellion.

Writing and conflict

Conflict and rebellion can perform a creative part in the formation of the writer when we learn how to use them. It is through the written word that the writer asserts the *difference* between herself or himself and other people and other writers. Philip Larkin (in *Required Writing*) said that part of the reason he wrote was that no one else had written what he wanted to read, and W. B. Yeats claimed that rhetoric emerges out of one's quarrel with other people and poetry out of the quarrel with oneself. The quarrels and conflicts we have buried within us also possess a rich fecundating power for the writer.

Think of your own favourite writer, of all the books she or he has written. Do you find knots of conflict that the writer keeps trying to unravel and then tie up again? Do you find that, as Adrienne Rich wrote of Marie Curie, 'her wounds came from the same source as her power?'

Spilling the knots from one's entrails out on to paper isn't likely to make a poem or story that others will want to read, but many writers do have to go through the 'spilling' process in order to know just what it is they have to hammer into shape. Words come out differently on paper from how we imagine them in our heads. We discover ourselves through the form of the sentence. The act of transforming our knots into marks on the paper begins to give a discipline. Something inside says 'You can't say it that way, it doesn't work' and so we change it. Even as we start to write, we find ourselves making contact with feelings for rhythm and style. Later we will revise the writing more stringently: pruning, shifting the weight, reordering, until every part holds every other part and it *stands*: it means what we want it to mean.

Getting ready to write

In his book *A Separate Reality*, Carlos Casteneda explores the importance of what he calls 'finding your spot' before you can begin to learn anything. Finding a place for one's writing work, both a practical place – a room in the house, a desk, a table, a comfortable chair – and a place in one's imagination are crucial prerequisites for enabling the writing voice to grow and develop. The writing self has to be nurtured. Remember that your chair is important. Just as you cannot live easily under a leaking roof, so you cannot write easily on a chair that is not right for you. Think about the light that is cast on your paper. Is it bright enough? Does it illuminate what you are doing properly? Think too about your paper. Colette bought well-finished paper that her pen could flow across easily. These things are not trivial. They are the material conditions of a writer's life, and they affect your writing.

When we first experience the desire to write, our writing voice may well be timid, weak, needy and underfed, so we need to feed it, to let the writer-self know that it is significant for us. We need to purposefully put time aside to spend with it, listen to it. The writer in us has to know that we are making it a priority, that we are prepared to let other obligations go in order to play with it, nourish it, accord it a central place in our lives. If, when I describe the writer-self, it sounds as though I am describing a baby, that is entirely intentional.

When you are getting ready to write, think carefully about what you need, about what will nourish the starveling child. Writing time is *your* time; you need to claim it for yourself, often against the demands of other people. Sometimes this may feel like a military strategy and it is quite in order to treat it this way: to plot and plan to take the fortress which is your imaginary castle, your silent, fertile abode, despite the background of your everyday tasks and obligations. When you begin to feel guilty, remind yourself that it's for the child's sake.

You may need to ask yourself questions like 'When am I likely to have some space to myself?', 'When is it likely to be quiet?', 'Do I need to leave the house or can I find time at home, when the others are out?', 'Can I work when there are other people around?' I find it wise to let people know that I am writing, that I need solitude. Others *do* learn to respect your need to be alone, if you persist in maintaining it. Remember that if you take this need seriously, others will come to accept it.

Opening the storehouse door

This is the first exercise in this book and in certain ways the most important. It constitutes your attempt to explore your writer-self, to find out its needs, its insecurities and its strengths. The aim of the exercise is to begin to discover why you relate to written language in the way you do and to trigger the first probings into your own, unique way of understanding yourself and your world. Ask yourself these questions:

- What are my earliest memories of speaking and writing?
- Whom do I remember talking to most as a child?
- Was it primarily a relationship of conflict or harmony?
- What do I remember about learning to write?
- What were the words I was not allowed to say?
- Do I have an early memory of *misunderstanding*, when something I said was misunderstood, perhaps with painful or embarrassing consequences, by a friend, a member of my family or a teacher?
- With whom did I feel most open and confident about expressing myself in words?
- Was there a difference between what I felt I could *say* and what I felt I could *write*?

These are hard questions to answer, so be prepared to take your time and dig deep. It's not a race or a competition, but a process of discovering, or uncovering, your own writing voice. Note down the first thoughts that come into your head and follow where they lead; but do try to answer all the questions.

When you've made the notes, structure them into two or three pages of narrative prose. Even if you want to make a poem in the end, write in prose first, just to make sure you're clear about the feelings and experiences that have come to the surface. Yeats wrote out his poems in prose first: it is a discipline which works. The whole exercise, from beginning to end, should take about two hours, with plenty of time at the start just for thinking. Be prepared to *centre* yourself in revery, to give yourself up to your memories just as your sleeping self gives itself up to a dream. Try to protect yourself from interruptions – but if an interruption is unavoidable, don't worry. Do what you have to do, but keep the memories with you, let them take root in your conscious mind while you're away from your desk. Interruptions are not always a curse; I sometimes find that a lost association breaks the surface for air precisely when I've stopped actively thinking about the writing. When you've made a physical space – a table and a chair – for your writer-self, you will find that an inner space begins to open up in the imagination. You will learn to hold your work with you even when you are prevented from doing it. Alexander Solzhenitsyn held much of his work in his mind while he was in a labour camp. He stored it up – the mind's ability to store is inexhaustible – and wrote it down when he was finally released. If *that* is possible, then you can certainly get through interruptions without fear of losing your load.

When you've finished writing, put it away for two or three days: leave it, don't look at it for a while. You are of course free to write anything else while you leave your first piece fallow. But while you have separated yourself from your own autobiographical work, take a look at the following extracts:

> She developed a method in her whippings: standing with her switch in her hand, she would order me to come before her. I would plead or cry or run away. But at last I had to come. Without taking hold of me, she forced me to stand in one spot of my own will, while she whipped me on all sides. Afterwards, when I continued to sob as children do, she would order me to stop or she would 'stomp me into the ground'.

I remember once that I could not and with one swoop she was upon me
– over the head, down the back, on my bare legs, until in agony and
terror I ran for the house screaming for my father. Yet what could I say
to my father – I was little and could not explain. And he would not
believe.

My mother continued to say that I lied. But I did not know it. I was
never clear. What was truth and what was fancy I could not know. To
me, the wind in the tree tops really carried stories on its back; the red
bird that came to our cherry tree told me things; the fat, velvety
flowers in the forest laughed and I answered; the little calf in the field
held long conversations with me.

But at last I learned to know what a lie was: to induce my mother to
stop beating me I would lie – I would say, yes, I had lied and was sorry,
and then she would whip me for having withheld the admission so long.
As time went on, to avoid a whipping, I learned to tell her only the
things I thought she wanted to hear.

'I have but one child who is stubborn and a liar, and that is Marie,'
she would tell strangers or neighbours. At first I was humiliated to tears;
later I became hardened; later still I accepted it as a fact and did not
even try to deny it.

It has been one of the greatest struggles of my life to learn to tell the
truth ...

                                   Agnes Smedley, *Daughter of Earth*

Remind me how we loved our mother's body
our mouths drawing the first
thin sweetness from her nipples

our faces dreaming hour on hour
in the salt smell of her lap. Remind me
how her touch melted childgrief

how she floated great and tender in our dark
or stood guard over us
against our willing

and how we thought she loved
the strange male body first
that took, that took, whose taking seemed a law

and how she sent us weeping
into that law
how we remet her in our childbirth visions

erect, enthroned, above

a spiral stair
and crawled and panted toward her

I know, I remember, but
hold me, remind me
of how her woman's flesh was made taboo to us

Adrienne Rich, 'Sibling Mysteries' in
The Dream of a Common Language

Both writers explore an early relationship, the conflict and misunderstanding within it and the terrible sense of loss which arises when one is deprived, in one sense or another, of one's mother. Agnes Smedley's heroine, Marie, talks about having to shut her mother out, shut off from her, in order to protect herself against her mother's extraordinary cruelty – while Adrienne Rich works on the feeling of severance, of being deprived of her mother in a culture which insists that the daughters turn away from the mother towards the father.

Your early experiences form a rich vein – the mother lode perhaps – from which you can learn to dig your finest material. What you do with it once you've brought it to the surface is another matter: it is enough for now that you acknowledge it is there and begin to discover ways of getting at it.

Your notebook

I think you will have found that this exercise produced more thoughts, images and ideas than you were able to use in what you finally wrote. Do not throw any of them away: writers make new garments out of castoffs all the time. Transfer all the thoughts and images you like into a notebook. The superflux will provide new material for you whenever ideas are not coming easily. Your notebook should be small enough to fit in your bag or pocket and have covers which are firm enough to prevent it from being damaged easily. Record in it anything you fancy: a new word, a new way of describing a colour, a particular action you saw performed which you'd like to describe in detail while it's fresh.

Your notebook is the tool which enables you to take any experience, any observation, any physical sensation and turn it into something which can be shared by others. In Anna Akhmatova's words, it forms a way of 'bearing witness to the common lot'. Every society requires its witnesses: those who are not afraid to render and preserve in words the range and scope of human experience for that time and that place. When Akhmatova stood in line for 17 months outside the gaol in Leningrad, waiting for news of her son, a woman, hearing her name, approached her and said, 'Can you describe this?' to which the poet returned: 'I can.' That woman *needed* the poet; a poem had to be written to ensure that her suffering, and that of numberless others, should not be dishonoured by silence. Writing is a way of honouring the world we live in, its living and its dead.

Writing with the whole self

New writers often say 'Well, I'm writing now. I've started. But when I look at what I've written, I feel it's not all there. There's a dimension missing, it has no depth.' I believe that the reason for this being such a common problem is that we live, in the Western industrialised world, in such a disembodied way. Half the time we carry on as if we didn't have a body: and we only think about our bodies if they trouble us – if we're hungry or in pain. When we are writing we must unlearn this disembodiedness if our work is to achieve the depth and richness we desire: we must learn to speak with our whole body and not just through our mind's eye. The eye is, after all, the most cerebral, least sensuous organ. If we wrote through our eyes alone, we would represent a silent world without smells, without tastes, without texture. I think you will find as you begin to write through *all* your senses, that your writing transforms itself into something more fully alive.

Do this next exercise and then try to *hold* all your senses in listening expectancy in your future writing. The exercise lasts for five days.

On the first day, concentrate only on your sense of touch. Think through your fingers, think through your skin. Be aware of every object, every texture, every current of air your body comes into contact with. Make the surface of your body alive to every stimulation, whether pleasant or not. Then, at the end of the day, write about five hundred words through your sense of touch. Hold on to all you have experienced in the day through your writing: write about everything you have touched.

On the second day, think through your sense of taste. As well as the obvious, known tastes of food and drink, stick your tongue out to discover what the air tastes like. Does rain have a taste? What does leather taste like – and the bricks of a house? Don't eat anything dangerous – but try to extend the range of things you know the taste of. In the evening, write about them.

On the third day, make your nose into your organ of chief intelligence. Imagine that you are a dog. What can you discover from the smells around you? Follow your nose – to explore the smells you cherish. What do you love to smell? What repels you? Hold on to all these smells until the evening, when you can deliver them up onto the blank paper.

Devote your fourth day to the sense of hearing. Don't worry about what people say, only about the tones of their voices, their cough, their indrawings of breath. Hear the road drill, the articulated lorry, the siren – really hear them. Don't shut them out as you normally do. And then – what do you love to hear? Why are your *beloved* sounds sweet to you? Again, write it all down at the end of the day.

Finally we come to sight, the most human of senses, the one which normally eclipses all the others. Look at movement – the movement of a walking body; look at colour, at light and its shifting patterns. Look at darkness. Look at everything. Then put it on paper in the evening.

Simile and metaphor

In the exercise above, you were probably using simile and metaphor without realising it. It will be useful to you to make your use of them conscious, primarily to avoid cliché, the worm in every writer's bud.

A simile is introduced by a word such as *like, as* or *such*. It forms a way of enriching description by comparing one thing with another. For example:

> My heart is like a singing bird.
>
> Christina Rossetti

The word metaphor comes from the Greek *metaphorá*, which means transference or 'to carry over'. It occurs when a writer applies a name or a descriptive term to an object to which it is not literally applicable; when a word is carried over from its normal use to a new use. For example:

> Boys and girls tumbling in the street, and playing, were moving jewels.
>
> Thomas Traherne

They weren't literally jewels but because of the flash and sparkle of their bodies they were metaphorically so.

Simile and metaphor, then, serve to form a bridge between the experience a writer wants to convey and the reader's own experience. Christina Rossetti wanted to convey a particular feeling of overwhelming joy. She did not say 'I feel overwhelming joy' but 'My heart is like a singing bird' which is infinitely more powerful. And why? I think because 'overwhelming joy' describes the experience in abstract terms. We know vaguely what she means, but we do not feel it for ourselves. We all know, though, how a singing bird makes us feel and we can imagine how the bird feels as it throws its song out into the air. Similarly with metaphor. Traherne does not write 'Boys and girls tumbling in the street, and playing, flashed this way and that, causing many reflecting lights which dazzled me'. That is just confusing. He forces us to conjure up something we can picture entirely for ourselves: the wild interplay of sparkling colours, shocking and pleasing, that occurs when jewels move. Both Rossetti and Traherne, through simile and metaphor, make the reader work harder. They compel the reader to give something of herself or himself to the text. It is this work, performed by the writer *and* reader, which ensures that the communication of feeling can take place.

At this point you should go through the exercise on the senses and underline where you have used either a simile or a metaphor. Write all your metaphors and similes down on a separate sheet of paper. The next stage is an important one in your ability to evaluate, assess and improve your own work. Go through each simile and each metaphor in turn and ask yourself: 'Have I heard this before? Is it too familiar, is it worn out? Or is it new?' If it is new and unfamiliar, you might experience a sense of physical pleasure. When I come across a new metaphor, one that stretches my understanding, I feel cold. I know that something new has happened, that I've been forced to make a connection I've never made before. If the simile or metaphor leaves you feeling exactly the same, if it doesn't move you, then you could improve it. Work now on making this aspect of your writing stronger, stranger, less expected. One word of warning. Your writing will become ridiculous if you cram metaphors together. Metaphors produce a clear effect on the reader but that effect will become confused and diminished if you use too many or if you mix them up, as in these lamentable examples:

> She is a budding star who already sings with a master hand.
> I smell a rat in the air: I shall nip it in the bud.

Consolidation

An enormous progress will have occurred over the course of these exercises – a progress which you should be aware of, feel and thoroughly take in. Look again at your first piece of writing. From that you began to make contact with the memories of conflict and strong feeling that will be invaluable in your future writing work. Then look at the five-day exercise on the senses: this has enabled you to start writing with the knowledge you derive from your whole body, rather than merely the abstract, visual knowledge you adduce through your eyes. It has caused you to discover for yourself Margaret Atwood's definition of metaphor:

> when ...
>   ... the word
> splits & doubles & speaks
> the truth & and body
> itself becomes a mouth.
>
>   'Spelling'

2   The Space we Inhabit

In this chapter I want to search with you for the spirit of place, to conjure up the spirit that will give life and breath to descriptions of places. I find that many new writers' stories and poems seem to occur in a spatial and social vacuum: the writer launches straight into an account of action, ideas, thoughts, feelings, without giving any clear sense of where all this is taking place. The result is that the reader feels lost – because the writer hasn't bothered to say where they are. It is frustrating, confusing and severely diminishes the pleasure the writing could bring. But if the place is *there*, living and breathing *through* what happens, then the writing achieves another dimension: it becomes more real:

> The present breaks our hearts. We lie and freeze,
> our fingers icy as a bunch of keys.
> Nothing will thaw these bones except
> memory like an ancient blanket wrapped
> about us when we sleep at home again,
> smelling of picnics, closets, sicknesses,
> old nightmare,
> > and insomnia's spreading stain.
> > > Adrienne Rich, 'Readings of History'

Even poetry, which seems to arise out of nowhere, requires its nest, its squatting place. Look at the image Adrienne Rich has used in her poem: that of home. She conjures up a place to balance against the freezing and breaking of the present. She appeals to our memory of shelter, our perpetual desire for it and fires our memory into longing with the ignition of 'blanket', 'picnics', 'sicknesses' and 'spreading stain'. How much is evoked by spreading stain! A glass of juice toppled onto a white tablecloth; blood dripping onto the carpet or linoleum; the *staining* of childhood by what we learn to fear. We can each supply our own particulars but the important point is that Rich has set us going with her place – her place that grows out of memory.

Now bring your own memories to bear. Clamber back in your mind to the house that meant most to you when you were small. I am going to offer you certain words: *threshold, attic, cellar, kitchen, bedroom, corridor.* Choose one or two of them. Take a blank sheet of paper and write down everything that occurs to you about the word(s) you have chosen, giving yourself about ten minutes.

Were you surprised at how much these words evoked for you, at the richness of feeling and detail they seemed to compel? This was the reason I asked you to return to the house of your childhood: because the places we have loved – or hated – as children remain in the mind as almost a structuring force. They become part of us, both consciously and unconsciously, determining our perceptions and our understanding. When we return to them with the scrutiny of our adult minds, they appear as towering shelters, full of colour and minutely remembered detail.

When the house of childhood does not serve as a place of support and nurture, when there is intense conflict between different members of the household, then we may find that many memories of *indoors* have been suppressed. If this is true in your own case, try a word like *window, garden* or *playground.* There may have been so much conflict indoors that you had to construct your shelter elsewhere. If, however, you can consciously remember conflicts or tensions inside the house, then go ahead with your writing work. Ask yourself: did conflict regularly occur in certain areas – at the kitchen table for example? I want you to concentrate on the way the rooms themselves bring about certain kinds of behaviour.

A note on ambiguity

You are likely to find that your memories of the house of childhood are split – into fear and security, fire and ice, harmony and conflict. Try to hold these contradictory memories together: don't give in to the temptation to simplify your experience by discarding one important aspect of it. You will find that your writing becomes thinner, poorer, less convincing if you take this easy way out. The courage to hold contradictory impressions together is a brave skill, highly prized by writers. John Keats called it 'negative capability' and it is akin to Ernest Hemingway's 'becoming strong in the broken places'. Michel de Montaigne was so convinced of the importance of contradictoriness that he had emblazoned on the domed ceiling of his library the motto: 'To Every Reason an Equal Reason can be opposed.' So do not be afraid to hold on to impressions that logically seem to cancel one another out.

At first you may have to represent this contradictoriness chronologically, in the manner of 'At first the corridor frightened me, but later I came to love it, its hatpegs, its long coats to hide behind.' With further practice you will discover words that hold more than one meaning, that are themselves ambiguous, enabling you to represent contending realities at a single stroke. Here is an example from *Antony and Cleopatra*, where Cleopatra is persuading the snake to bite and kill her:

> Come, thou mortal wretch,
> With thy sharp teeth this knot intrinsicate
> Of life at once untie. Poor venomous fool,
> Be angry, and dispatch.
>
> Act V, Scene ii

The ambiguous words here are *mortal, intrinsicate* and *dispatch*. *Mortal* means both that the snake is mortal, will have a life and then die, and also that it is capable of dealing a mortal blow, of killing. *Intrinsicate* is a deliberately created ambiguity, a made-up word designed to contain two words: intricate and intrinsic. Shakespeare uses it to make us feel how complex and deeply inward is the knot of life, the knot which, while it remains tied, causes Cleopatra to be alive rather than dead. The snake will untie the intricate knot and the deeply hidden force of life within Cleopatra will cease. *Dispatch* contains the sense of 'to get on with something', haste, and also 'to do away with', to polish off, to send off to the next life.

Be aware of the ambiguities in your own writing. When, reading over your work, you discover one, ask yourself whether or not you intended it. Does it add another dimension? Or is it merely vague? There is a great divide between ambiguity and vagueness. Think how irritated you would be if you began reading a story with the opening sentence 'They were cooking apples.' Does the 'they' refer to the apples or the cooks? It is an unnecessary vagueness that demands clarification. When you question yourself about whether a phrase is ambiguous or vague, the litmus test is usually 'Did I intend it be written that way? Does that phrase need to be ambiguous?'

Living room, writing room

How can you use your descriptions of place – a room, a garden bench, the large cupboard under the stairs, a lift in a block of flats – to create a mood strong enough to sustain your story? For events do not take place spontaneously, out of nowhere; they come to fullness as a result of many active forces. And the place is not simply the background or backdrop against which the action occurs; it plays its part in the drama.

Look at this description of a place and try to guess some of the action of the story from it:

> They arrive at the empty basement flat just after one. She dumps the baby straight into his cot. He is wet and hungry, but also tired. And so is she. They cry themselves to sleep, he behind his wooden bars and she on the big sagging bed. The peeling wallpaper, damp-stained and stinking of mould, decorates her dreams. She awakes to the sight of mildew spreading beneath the window-sill. The odour of must and the small waking cry of a child seep into the air.
>
> Sandra Warne, 'All in a Row'

I think you will agree that the physical scene determines the atmosphere of the writing, which in its turn determines what will happen, the action of the story. I am making a very simple point: that the material conditions of our lives and our characters' lives shape, to a large extent, the way those lives progress. We know this from experience; it seems so obvious that it is not even worth saying. But if we omit those material conditions from our writing, then the writing voice loses much of its authority and power. The reader senses that one large cause of events is missing.

Spend some time considering the effect of your own living conditions upon your writing. Under what circumstances do you write most easily? What prevents you from writing? Consider too the circumstances of Jane Austen, whose novels breathe such grace and balance that we assume she wrote with no distractions:

> 'How she was able to effect all this', her nephew writes in his Memoir, 'is surprising, for she had no separate study to repair to, and most of the work must have been done in the general sitting-room, subject to all kinds of casual interruptions. She was careful that her occupation

should not be suspected by servants or visitors or any persons beyond
her own family party.'

J. E. Austen, *Memoir of Jane Austen*

Although the nephew may have exaggerated his aunt's powers of concentration – Lizzie and Jane in *Pride and Prejudice* each have a room
of their own and servants to build a fire for them – there is no doubt
that our working conditions do influence the quality of our writing.
The place, in this too, plays its part.

Conjuring up the spirit of place

Imagine yourself in a room you love. Close your eyes so you can walk
into it. In revery, walk around your room. Cast your eyes around
slowly; dwell on each object. Imagine yourself picking one or two of
these objects up. How do they feel next to your skin? How do they
smell? Allow yourself to become open and spongy, soak up the atmosphere and objects in the room until you feel drenched by them.

This room might exist in your house or flat or only in your imagination. But whether it is real or imaginary, it should be something of an
ideal, a place where you feel secure and protected. I want you to think
of it as the room where you do your writing. When you have spent
about ten minutes in quiet revery, describe the beloved room.

The place you've just written about helps you to feel at ease, to feel
nourished, warm, loved. It helps you to feel like a whole person: integrated, centred, in some important way *satisfied*. Remember that,
even if no such room exists for you, you have written as though it
does. What you have started to do is create this place of support and
satisfaction in yourself: you've begun to *make room* in your mind for
your writer-self.

Now read your writing through. How do you feel when you read it?
Emily Dickinson defined writing that *works* as 'something that makes
me feel as though the top of my head is coming off'. She said she knew
of no other way to assess the value of a piece. You can measure your
own writing in this way, too. Ask yourself these questions:

> Have I written all I wanted to write about the room, or have I left out
> something important? How do I feel when I read it – elated, stretched,
> sad, longing ...? Or do I simply feel the same?

If the writing doesn't have a tangible effect on you, the writer, it is unlikely to stir or arouse others.

Reworking and strengthening

Now it is time to focus in detail upon your description. Take two felt-tip pens, of different colours, and underline in one colour all the words that catch the meaning you intended, that evoke strongly the feelings you have about the room. With the other pen, underline the parts you are not satisfied with, the phrases that fall short of expressing your meaning. Remember that you are your own best critic and only you can finally decide what it is you wanted to say.

Make a list on a separate sheet of paper of the flabby, vague, unfocused parts, so you can look at them out of context. What is it about them that dissatisfies you? Have you used words that are too familiar, worn-out similes, too many abstract nouns? As I go through some of the possible problems, check back to see which of them apply to the slack parts of your own writing.

Abstract nouns

These are words like 'joy', 'truth', 'misery', 'reflection', 'beauty' and 'ingratitude': naming words for states of mind, intellectual concepts and categories. They are not words for physical things, like objects or parts of the body, but for states or processes that we cannot physically see or feel. Consequently, these words mean quite different things to different people. In creative writing they often only do half the job you used them for: they say more or less what you mean, but not exactly. For example, to write that you feel joyful in the room is a kind of vague shorthand. It reminds *you* how you felt there but leaves the reader with unanswered questions. The reader would have a much fuller impression of your state of mind if you lovingly evoked, say, the feel of a rug under your feet, the texture of the curtains, the smell of a shawl. Bringing in these things would make the room real to the reader – and new to you, the writer, because you'd have recreated it, having laid each of your senses open to it. The writing then becomes tangible, concrete, unique, instead of vague and hard to grasp.

Adjectives

Adjectives describe nouns. They give us extra knowledge about the thing itself. Here are some examples:

> a *fierce* temper
> a *moving* story
> a *bitter* quarrel
> an *old* man

You will notice that the adjectives in this list are, to put it bluntly, boring. We've heard them so many times that they've ceased to have any effect. Check your work for boring adjectives. When you find one, ask yourself 'Do I really need *this* word or would the noun work better on its own? Can I find a noun that would convey the sense more clearly?' You may find that you do need an adjective, but not that one. When searching for the right adjective, bear in mind that your effect on the reader will be stronger if you can create a physical sensation, if you can make the reader conjure up a colour, a texture, a smell or a sound, rather than using a word like 'soothing', or 'lovely' or (worst of all) 'evocative'. Say, for example, there is a smell in the room that reminds you of your childhood. Don't be tempted to describe it as 'reminiscent' or 'reassuring'. Say exactly what the smell is. Is it mothballs or furniture polish or tobacco or vapour rub? If you 'give' the smell to the reader rather than using your own private shorthand, then the reader's own nose will do the work. The reader will smell the smell with you, with real participation and pleasure, rather than having to resentfully take your word for it. Also, you may find that in taking this concrete approach, you are making your nouns work harder for you and using fewer adjectives. This, again, will make your writing firmer, more substantial.

Adverbs

Adverbs describe verbs in the same way that adjectives describe nouns. They usually end in '-ly'. For example:

> I walked *slowly* into the room.
> *Lovingly* I touched the curtains.
> I held the vase *carefully*.

Adverbs and adjectives contain similar problems: they both prevent the verb or the noun doing all the work it is capable of and rob a phrase of its necessary precision. Adverbs often do not render exactly *how* an action took place. Compare these sentences with the examples above:

> I edged into the room.
> I sidled into the room. Which was it?
>
> I fondled the curtains.
> I caressed the curtains. Which was it?
>
> I lifted the vase between my thumb and forefinger.
> I grasped the vase with both hands. Which was it?

Different verbs offer alternative meanings in each of these sentences. They are all more exact than the sentences that rely on adverbs.

On the other hand, when adjectives and adverbs appear in clusters, they can produce a necessary *ritardando*. They force the reader to slow down, to dwell or brood on what is happening. They stop the eye from moving so fast, as in these sentences:

> *Silently* I circled the desk, pacing, prowling. *Wooden, solid*, it seemed to catch my eye, with its *open, cleared* space, its *black, inviting* pen.

You can see the way the italic words, the adverb and adjectives, work to hold the reader still, locking their gaze upon the desk, which then seems to hypnotise both writer and reader.

Conversing with the spirits of place

There is a kind of mystical, powerful writing which does not simply evoke the spirit of place in order to determine action but seeks to converse with it, enter into a dialogue with all that has gone before. There is a kind of writing which lets the spirits of place speak. This writing may at first seem strange because it aims beyond the physical reality of our senses – addressing the past, the future and the spirits of those who are before and after. I want to write about it here so that new writers will know it exists and perhaps be brave enough to address this difficult aspect of our experience in their work.

In *The Color Purple*, Alice Walker, through the letters of Nettie, a young black woman who has accompanied two missionaries to the home of the Olinka tribe in Africa, writes of the healing, life-giving qualities of the roofleaf plant, which embodies the spirit of place for the tribe:

> The people prayed to their gods and waited impatiently for the seasons to change. As soon as the rain stopped they rushed to the old roofleaf beds and tried to find the old roots. But of the endless numbers that had always grown there, only a few dozen remained. It was five years before the roofleaf became plentiful again. During those five years many more in the village died. Many left, never to return. Many were eaten by animals. Many, many were sick. The chief was given all his storebought utensils and forced to walk away from the village forever. His wives were given to other men.
>
> On the day when all the huts had roofs again from the roofleaf, the villagers celebrated by singing and dancing and telling the story of the roofleaf. The roofleaf became the thing they worship.
>
> Looking over the heads of the children at the end of this tale, I saw slowly coming towards us, a large brown spiky thing as big as a room, with a dozen legs walking slowly and carefully under it. When it reached our canopy, it was presented to us. It was our roof.
>
> As it approached, the people bowed down.
>
> The white missionary before you would not let us have this ceremony, said Joseph. But the Olinka like it very much. We know a roofleaf is not Jesus Christ, but in its humble way, is it not God?
>
> So there we sat, Celie, face to face with the Olinka God. And Celie, I was so tired and sleepy and full of chicken and groundnut stew, my ears ringing with song, that all that Joseph said made perfect sense to me.

In *i is a long memoried woman*, Grace Nichols builds a stunning sequence of poems out of just such a search for an imaginative resting place. Her memory ploughs back, past the beginning of her own life, to Africa and slavery, to Guyana, sugar, punishment on the plantation, loyalty and betrayal. Through the story runs the gold thread of religion and magic:

> alligator teeth
> and feathers
> old root and powder
>
> I kyan not work this craft
> this magic black
> on my own strength
>
> 'Omen'

a thread which visibly supports the poet's intercessions with the spirits of her past. Through the search over three continents, homelessness and pain-memory, she is able to find a new tongue as the last poem, in a sort of quiet, cautious exultation, shows. I want to stress this connection between searching for home and finding a tongue, a writing voice, because I believe it to be fundamental to your own writing development.

A new angle of vision

In the exercise you are now about to attempt you will begin to see a familiar place through unfamiliar eyes. Your aim in this writing is to penetrate and supervene the way you normally see and construe your surroundings, to discover a new angle of vision. You may be unsympathetic to the transcendental or spiritual interpretations of reality in the writings I have just cited: that doesn't matter. I have written about them to show that spiritual journeys and beliefs are legitimate, fruitful ways of exploring the world and to encourage writers to go ahead with this kind of exploration if they so wish. If you do not wish to do so, then there are many other new angles of vision available to you: a child's viewpoint, for example, an animal's or the viewpoint of a stranger who may interpret familiar customs in unfamiliar ways. The painter Jean-Baptiste Chardin shatters our 'knowledge' of the world by presenting it to us in a new way, as if we were children and his bowl of fruit stood just above our eye-level. This 'newness', which is not really new but more an expansion of the rigid barriers of the individual self so that we see something as if we were not ourselves, is, I believe, one of the attributes of authentic, pleasurable art.

This exercise can be approached in one of two ways:

- Take a familiar place and describe it through unfamiliar eyes.
- Write about a journey to an unfamiliar place, a place that, when you visited it, fractured, ruptured or enlarged your understanding of the world.

Before you begin to write, think over what you have learned from the previous exercise. Think about clichés, abstract nouns, adjectives and adverbs. As you are trying to find a new angle of vision, it is particularly important that you avoid familiar or worn-out ways of writing.

Although I am reluctant to lay down rules, I do find the following guidelines, set out in H. W. & F. G. Fowlers' *The King's English*, helpful as a sort of mental checklist for my own work:

1 Prefer the familiar word to the far-fetched.
2 Prefer the concrete word to the abstract.
3 Prefer the single word to the circumlocution.
4 Prefer the Saxon word to the Romance.
5 Prefer the short word to the long.

It is not necessary to stick rigidly to these. But if you do use a far-fetched or archaic word like *valetudinarian*, for example, as Jane Austen did on the first page of *Emma*, be sure you know why you are using it. Be sure, first, that no other word will do.

If you look closely at the Fowlers' five 'prefers', you will find that they are trying to guide you away from fancy writing. It is difficult to accept such guidance because often, in school, we are misled into thinking that fancy writing is good writing. We learn, mistakenly, that good writing is obscure, dense and full of hard words. We come to believe that good writing shows how clever we are. But when we read a page of powerful writing, we see immediately that it is not clever and has nothing to do with fanciness or obscurity. It uses plain words to their fullest effect so that we are stunned by how much the writer has enabled them to mean. When Maxim Gorki as a young man read a story by Guy de Maupassant, he marvelled 'why the plain, familiar words put together by a man into a story about the uninteresting life of a servant moved me so'.

Look at this section from Adrienne Rich's poem 'In the Wake of Home':

> But you will be drawn to places
> where generations lie
> side by side with each other:
> fathers, mothers and children
> in the family prayerbook
> or the country burying-ground
> You will hack your way through the bush
> to the Jodensavanne
> where the gravestones are black with mould
> You will stare at old family albums

with their smiles their resemblances
You will want to believe that nobody
wandered off became strange
no woman dropped her baby and ran
no father took off for the hills
no axe splintered the door
– that once at least it was in order
and nobody came to grief

Note how simply Adrienne Rich says what she has to say. There is no superflux, no trailing extras: only a piercing representation of the constant search for the secure, good-enough home, the search that we persist in despite endless disappointment and frustration.

Note the startling sparsity of adjectives: she uses them only when she is forced to, so they seem pressed out of the nouns through sheer weight of need. Look at these adjectives: *family, country, black, old, strange*. They are tough, tensile; part of the structure of the poem rather than decorative vines creeping around it. Note particularly the total absence of adverbs. The verbs do their own work. They don't need to lean on an adverb for greater clarity.

Bring all you have learned to bear on the exercise. Find a place to write, a room, and make room for your writer-self in your mind.

3   Bringing your Descriptions to Life

Close your eyes and sit quietly.
Bring into your inner field of vision – a lemon.
Examine it closely.
It is porous, with a little green dot in the middle of each pore.
Feel the knobbly, cool surface.
Imagine a knife.
You are slicing the lemon in half.
You raise one half to your mouth and sink your teeth into it.
What has happened?

This is an experiment suggested by José Silva and Philip Miele. I'll wager that your salivary glands started pumping out liquid as you imagined yourself biting into the lemon. The lemon became real for you; your imagination tricked your body into believing it would have to cope with a mouthful of pure citrus. That is one of the things that writing does: it entices the reader into an 'unreal' world, a world 'really' only composed of funny marks on a page, and through those marks makes the reader consider something which may form no part of normal life. It throws words like *real* and *normal* into question, continually challenges and subverts the things we take for granted, the things we think we know.

As you work on the exercises in this chapter, I want you to hold the lemon up steadily, as a pole star. It engendered a physical response. Make that a central aim in your descriptive writing.

Here is a passage by Colette. As you read it, be aware of how it makes you feel:

The caterpillar was perhaps asleep, moulded to the form of a supporting twig of box thorn. The ravages about her testified to her vitality. There were nothing but shreds of leaves, gnawed stems, and barren shoots. Plump, as thick as my thumb and over four inches long, she swelled the fat rolls of her cabbage-green body, adorned at intervals with hairy warts of turquoise blue. I detached her gently from her twig and she writhed in anger, exposing her paler stomach and all her spiky little paws that clung leechlike to the branch to which I returned her.

'But, mother, she has devoured everything!'

The grey eyes behind the spectacles wavered perplexedly from the denuded twigs to the caterpillar and hence to my face: 'But what can I do about it? And after all, the box thorn she's eating, you know, is the one that strangles honeysuckle.'

'But in any case, what can I do about it? I can hardly kill the creature.'

The scene is before me as I write, the garden with its sun-warmed walls, the last of the black cherries hanging on the tree, the sky webbed with long pink clouds. I can feel again beneath my fingers the vigorous resentment of the caterpillar, the wet, leathery hydrangea leaves, and my mother's little work-worn hand.

I can evoke the wind at will and make it rustle the stiff papery blades of the bamboos and sing, through the comb-like leaves of the yew, as a worthy accompaniment to the voice that on that day and on all other days, even to the final silence, spoke words that had always the same meaning.

'That child must have proper care. Can't we save that woman? Have those people got enough to eat? I can hardly kill the creature.'

My Mother's House

Look at the adjectives that apply to the caterpillar: *plump, thick, fat, cabbage-green, hairy, turquoise blue, spiky, leechlike.* Colette works at marshalling our feelings of revulsion at this voracious creature who has almost killed the poor box thorn. It is 'as thick as my thumb' – too big, surely. It must be a monster. She is setting her reader up to want the caterpillar dead. But then we witness a sudden turn. The child Colette starts speaking to her mother, lamenting the destruction of the plants. It is the dialogue with the mother that performs the crucial shift, enabling the reader to see the caterpillar in a new way, through the mother's loving intercession. It is her nurturing, sustaining toler-ance, extended, it seems, to all the creatures in the garden, that gives the initially repulsive caterpillar permission to live, permission to carry on denuding the box thorn.

Colette's universe is tactile, first and last. The little girl *holds* the caterpillar, plies it carefully from the twig to which it had *moulded* itself. The mother's eyes *waver* on her daughter's face, seeming to caress it. The sun has *warmed* the walls of the garden, the cherries *hang* on the tree. The writer *can feel again* the caterpillar, the hydrangea leaves and 'my mother's little work-worn hand'. Everything touches, everything depends on everything else. So her verbs are determinant in the making of her effects. But perhaps more important are the adjectives. I have discouraged the use of adjectives in the last two chapters but here you can see them used with superb skill. Colette positively revels in them. She often appends two to a single noun (*long pink clouds; wet, leathery hydrangea leaves; stiff papery blades*) to flesh out, give further fullness to the feeling she wants to call forth in the reader.

Another part of Colette's method of *making round,* making substantial, is her habit of moving backwards and forwards, towards and away from the object. In this piece she starts very near, so near she makes us want to vomit at the sight of the caterpillar, and then she slowly moves away, gaining emotional balance as she gains physical distance. She is able to tell us more because she refuses to stand still. And just as she will not keep the caterpillar restricted to one plane of vision, so also she avoids obsessively restricting herself to the object. She allows her mind to wander, following the associations that the caterpillar calls up, in a kind of trance, knowing they will lead her to where she needs to go.

Robert Lowell talked about the importance of this risk-taking, this following of the associative details, when he was interviewed for *Paris Review:*

> Almost the whole problem of writing poetry is to bring it back to what you really feel, and that takes an awful lot of manoeuvring. You may feel the doorknob more strongly than some big personal event, and the doorknob will open into something that you can use as your own. A lot of poetry seems to me very good in the tradition, but it doesn't move me very much because it doesn't have personal vibrance to it. I probably exaggerate the value of it, but it's precious to me. Some little image, some detail you've noticed – you're writing about a little country shop, just describing it, and your poem ends up with an existentialist account of your experience. But it's the shop that started it off. You didn't know why it meant a lot to you. Often images and often the sense of the beginning and the end of a poem are all you have – some journey to be gone through between those things – you know that, but you don't know the details.

You have to take the risk of describing the doorknob, or the little country shop, because they may be the only details that can take you in – into the strange and wonderful labyrinth that is your writer-self. They may be the clew to take you into what you didn't think you wanted to say.

In Chapter 2 we embarked on the task of building a house for the writer-self, a beloved abode where the writer in you can live. Now it is time to bring movement and activity into those secure, quiet recesses. Bring a part of your own body into the house and watch how it moves.

The hand

You could probably use any part of your body for this exercise, but I suggest you start with your hand, your writing hand. Look at it. Place it on the table in front of you. Hold it in the air. Survey it on both sides. Clench it into a fist, then open it out. Look at it close up, then at a distance. Smell it. Feel it.

Here are a few words, all associated with the hand:

Mount of Venus	callus	ring	knuckle
phalange	scar	vein	life-line

You will find many others as you search your mind and, later, your dictionary.

As you explore your hand, allow your mind to wander over the significance of all its markings. Is there a scar? Where did it come from? What are the nails like and the cuticles? Let your hand tell you about yourself. Follow the clues on the hand.

Now write a description of your hand, taking the risks, following the associations that may lead nowhere but are more likely to lead exactly where you need to go. Write for as long as you can. Then rest. Leave yourself time to regain energy before starting the second part of the exercise. Imagine several movements your hand habitually makes – like holding a saw, peeling potatoes, rubbing in cream or making a pot of tea. How does your hand move? What does the state and movement of the hand indicate about its owner? Again, you need to make the hand do the telling, rather than bring in any extra information from outside.

When you have completed the whole exercise, scrutinise it, paying particular attention to your adjectives. The exercise in Chapter 1 questioned the use of these seductive parts of speech, so you will be healthily suspicious of their allure. But you have also read the passage from Colette and felt the sensuous materiality of the physical world she evokes with her adjectives, so you know too how strong an effect they can produce. With these two seemingly contradictory attitudes in mind, underline all the adjectives you've used. Look at each one in turn. Does it add a new dimension to its noun or would the noun be better off without it? Does it make you *feel* the meaning of the noun more fully? Is it a necessary part of the structure of your sentence? In Colette's description we have the sentence: 'There were nothing but shreds of leaves, gnawed stems and barren shoots.' The adjectives here are *gnawed* and *barren* and they are both structurally crucial to the meaning of the sentence: the sentence needs them. To test whether or not you need an adjective, all you have to do is reduce your sentence to the form of a telegram. Take it down to the bone, to as few words as possible. Which of the following would be more accurate?

a)   nothing stems and shoots.
b)   gnawed stems barren shoots.
c)   shreds stems shoots.

In (a) the 'nothing' seems to contradict the 'stems and shoots' and in (c) the 'shreds stems shoots' simply does not make sense. We have to agree that Colette could not have done without her adjectives. Try to keep this exercise in your mind as you test out the necessity of your own adjectives.

Movement in the English sentence

For the second part of the exercise, you explored the sense of your hand in motion. Did you find this hard, harder than your description of the hand when it was still? Many writers, at first, feel frustrated and dissatisfied with this aspect of their work, rather as an archer does when he is learning to hit a moving target. If this is true for you, it may be worth considering the movement that lies immanent in every English sentence.

The English language is structured around its verbs. In each sentence, the subject and object are hinged together by the connecting verb, the verb that shows just what the subject is doing to the object:

> She brought the hammer down on the nail.

We have the subject – she, the object – the hammer, and the indirect object – the nail. The nail is an indirect object because it is related to the verb through the preposition – on. It is the verb 'to bring down' that forges the link between the otherwise *still* nouns and pronoun in the sentence. Without the verb they would be doing nothing. With the verb, we know that *she* is bringing the hammer down, and that the nail is being hammered. The verb calls all the nouns into a relationship of movement. From the Middle Ages to the present our language has hinged together the words that represent people, animals and things through verbs, through doing words. A verb always makes a link and it always represents some kind of movement.

That's all very well, you may object, but how do I make my verbs strong? How do I elicit a sense of bold movement in my sentences? I think Melquiadez, the gypsy in Gabriel García Márquez's *A Hundred Years of Solitude*, gives an answer when he says: 'Things have a life of their own. ... It's simply a matter of waking up their souls.' For you as writer, this entails looking so hard at the world you write about that you begin to feel the minute, imperceptible movements within it and learn to give them their most appropriate names. Notice, for example, in the sentences quoted above, how Márquez uses the verb 'waking up' before the object 'souls'. He does not say 'It's simply a matter of showing their souls' or 'bringing out their souls'. Those verbs, although roughly appropriate, evoke no tingle of recognition in the reader: they are flat, inert. In 'waking up their souls' Márquez cuts straight to the heart of our earliest desires: to rise from the dead and be reunited with the souls of our lost ones, our dead forebears. 'Waking up' associates with new life, a new day, rousing from sleep, a new beginning. It is therefore an immensely energetic, hopeful verb – and because our states of mind are influenced, without our conscious knowledge, by the language that surrounds us, this energy and hope is 'fed' to us through the verb.

If you have enough living movement in your writing, if your nouns support each sentence and your verbs fly, like flung ropes shaking cobwebs, between them, *then* you are in a position to decorate it with

adjectives and adverbs – but not until. If you load up your sentence
with trifles before you've built it properly, it will of course fall down.
William Carlos Williams made a lovely poem from this advice about
architectural structure. It begins:

> Rather notice, mon cher,
> that the moon is
> tilted above
> the point of the steeple
> than that its colour
> is shell-pink.

'To a Solitary Disciple'

It is the angle of the moon and its position in relation to the steeple,
rather than its colour, that is important to the poet. 'Shell-pink' would
give a prettiness to the poem but a prettiness that is inappropriate
because at this moment the moon has no connection with shells and
every connection with the lines of the steeple.

It is hard to know for sure why this is so, why this firmness of
outline is so important for the reader. When poetry, the oldest form of
writing (apart from household accounts) came into being, it was
written to serve a purpose: Sappho's lyrics entertained the guests at
wedding parties; the bravery of warriors was celebrated in song to
encourage the others and thrill the attendant crowds. Our word *verse*
comes from the Latin *vers*, which means *furrow*. A verse covers a span
of time, as does the ploughing of a furrow. People sang songs (lyric
poetry simply meant songs accompanied by the lyre) while ploughing, scything, threshing and grinding corn. The song was a part of the
day, a way of getting through the day tunefully, in rhythm. Perhaps
the origins of song help to explain why we still require a firm outline.
Decorative details add further delight only if the outline has achieved
its sure balance.

I think we still want our songs (poetry, story, play) to enable us to
get through the day tunefully, to afford some new angle of vision that
will 'give' us the world in a new way, elicit our love for the world
again, although our faculties may be tired, although the world may be
desolated. And the writer can only conjure up this gift for the reader if
he/she is prepared, first of all, to write plainly what he/she believes to
be true, rather than fall for the surface sweetmeats which seem to
satisfy but which, like sugar, leave the reader hungry minutes later.

Hemingway said, rightly I think: 'The most essential gift for a good writer is a built-in, shock-proof, shit detector. This is the writer's radar and all great writers have had it.' For 'shit' we can also read 'sugar' or 'soap' of the 'opera' variety. Some readers have grown accustomed to reading/watching/eating shit because they have never been offered anything else. This is an unspeakable tragedy. As a writer, your sovereign responsibility is to produce real food by making truthful representations. The first poets played their part in the making of bread: today's writers grow a different kind of food but still provide a nourishment neither they nor their readers can do without.

Cutting it down to the bone

During the fourteenth century, Japanese poets began to develop the form of verse we now call the haiku. Haiku literally means 'starting verse' because it was originally the beginning of an older verse form called the *tanka*. They are the sparest verses imaginable, so short that there is no room for anything but the concentrated feeling. Because of their brevity, Japanese students of poetry and religion are given the task of reading and writing haiku. One of the aims of the haiku writer is to avoid 'putting words between the truth and ourselves', to write the 'transparent' poetry that T. S. Eliot strove for, poetry that tries to close the distance between the word and the object it represents.

Words are not things: we have to accept that. There is a perilous gap between the table I write on and the word 'table'. The writer works at the impossible task of creating a poem, a narrative, which tries to narrow the gap between the signal and what is signalled: tries to reverse the separation between the world and what we write about the world. This effort to unite what cannot be united lies at the heart of the haiku and accounts for some of its tense, sad loveliness.

Here are three haiku from Matsuo Bashō, an early master of the form:

> The beginning of all art:
> a song when planting a rice field
> in the country's inmost part.

> On a journey, ill,
> and over fields all withered, dreams
> go wandering still.

> 'Leaving the house of a friend'
> out comes the bee
> from deep among peony pistils –
> oh, so reluctantly!

As you can see, although each of these poems 'simply' describes a moment that has something to do with the natural world, other thoughts and messages come through at the same time. The haiku poets aimed to condense many meanings into each phrase, so that the poem should speak of something that has both a particular and a general significance.

It is this degree of concentration I want you to work towards, using the haiku both as a point of departure and as a discipline you frequently return to. These are the formal dimensions of the haiku: five syllables in the first line; seven in the second; five in the third. The form can be made more flexible in English (the translator of Bashō has bent the rules considerably) because it does not possess the same internal formal necessity as it would in Japanese, but try to stick roughly to the proposed number of syllables. Your own haiku can have 'movement' as its subject, 'my town', 'spring' or whatever has moved you to powerful feeling. It can be funny or sad. You can experiment with the creation of different tones and moods in your three allotted lines.

Below are a few haiku written by students in a writing class. I include them here to encourage you to write about anything at all. Among the qualities for which Bashō's haiku are revered are 'a desire to use every instant to the uttermost; an appreciation of this even in natural objects; a feeling that nothing is alone, nothing unimportant; a wide sympathy; and an acute awareness of relationships of all kinds, including that of one sense to another.' Notice the verbs in the haiku below and the way they catch the emotion of a single moment:

> 'Thirteen floors up'
> if you fall
> off the balcony
> you've had it
> Smaaack!

> Nigel Young

I need to kiss you.
You must be joking, she said,
Out here, in the street?

Blowing top notes
She lifts her trombone up high
I watch her breathless.

He is everywhere
This younger greedy brother
Wanting to join in.

                                          Mel Kathchild

4 Making your Characters Speak

Writers often come to the problem of dialogue in fear and trembling. 'How do I make people speak naturally?' 'What would they say here?' 'What would he keep to himself there?' In our everyday lives we learn about people in many ways: the way they eat, their clothes, their scent, their movements, the way they hold themselves. But speech is one of the most revealing aspects of a person. We listen to the tone of their voice. Does it rankle and jar or do we feel at home with the sound? In Britain we often listen for a person's accent. It tells us where they come from. Often it tells us about their background or which social group they identify with. A dialect, too, where syntax and grammar work differently to 'standard' English, the sort taught in our educational institutions, shows that someone has consciously or unconsciously chosen not to abandon the speech patterns of their region for the blander cadences of BBC English.

We tend to assess people through what they say and the way they say it, to come to conclusions about whether we will like someone from the way they present themselves in words. D. H. Lawrence does it in a poem called 'The Oxford Voice'.

> When you hear it languishing
> and hooing and cooing and sidling through the
> front teeth,
> the Oxford voice
> or worse still
> the would-be Oxford voice
> you don't even laugh any more, you can't.

Here is Lawrence's anger, disciplined into a poem, about an accent and a quality of voice that speaks its own privilege and superiority. To write this poem, Lawrence evidently had to listen very hard to the

Oxford voice. He knows what happens inside the mouth and how the sounds are emitted. He *gives* us the voice, so we can examine it ourselves and ask our own questions about it, even though he does not cite directly anything the Oxford voice says. I think that Lawrence gives us our first clue in the writing of dialogue: that we must listen and, having listened, ask ourselves how we feel about the voice we've just heard.

We need to know how we feel about the sounds because if a certain accent or tone is anathema to us we often instinctively turn away from it, forget it. We make it impossible to use, when in fact that voice might greatly strengthen our writing. Also, if we turn away uncritically from a voice we hate or fear, then we are turning away from a source of conflict – and conflict is one of the writer's richest foods. If you can hold your feelings and examine them, force yourself to hear the voice and ask why it produces the response that it does, you are beginning to get the better of it, to break the fearful silence that surrounds it and, incidentally, to add another voice to your writing repertoire. Take this case, for example. One afternoon while I was in the USA, I received four obscene telephone calls. I was alone in the house and extremely frightened. When I called the police, they instructed me to write down everything the caller had said. I didn't want to. I just wanted to forget it had ever happened. But I forced myself to write it all down and, as I wrote it, it began to lose its power over me. I was containing the threats in written words: I was taking control. I kept the piece of paper and, after I returned home and thought more about the episode, I transformed it into a poem. It was important to me not to be silenced by the fear the anonymous caller invoked. After I'd finished the poem I felt triumphant that I'd broken my fear-silence. I also thought I'd written a better poem because I'd struggled with the voice, forced myself to hear it again in my mind and to reply to it. This dialogue went into the poem.

The voice of the place

If you come from a certain town or region, you will know what the different voices mean better than someone who comes from outside because you've learned the code. Some South American students, for whom English was a second or third language, found it impossible to read and understand Lawrence's play *The Daughter-in-Law*, a play where the use of Eastwood dialect renders it only easily accessible to those at home with varieties of regional English. *You* have to decide how much dialect will go into your writing and to do this you must be sure of your subject and know how wide you want your audience to be. Lawrence could express the strongest emotion through dialogue that used dialect – as in this section from *John Thomas and Lady Jane*:

> He looked at her still with a touch of resistance.
> 'I don't *care*!' she said. 'I'll give you all the money tomorrow, and let you buy what you like, if you'll take it.'
> 'No no!' he said, sinking into sullen silence. Then he looked up suddenly, beginning in a harsh voice, then breaking suddenly into broad dialect: 'I love – Ah luv thee! Ah luv thee!' He took her hand and pressed it against his belly. 'But tha wunna want ter ma'e me feel sma', shall ter? Let me be mysen, and let me feel as if tha' wor littler than me! dunna ma'e me feel sma', an' *down*! – else I canna stop wi' thee. Let me luv thee my own road, as if I was bringin' the money 'ome. I canna help it. Tha can laugh at me – but dunna want ter ma'e me feel sma'! Laugh at me – I like thee ter laugh at me! But be nice to me, an' dunna be big! For I feel I've got no place in the world, an' no mortal worth to nobody, if not to thee. An' I dunna want ter hate everything. It ma'es me feel as if I'd swallowed poison, an' had a bellyful, in a way.

Notice that Parkin is able to say what he truly means only after he has broken into dialect. It is as though Lawrence was acknowledging that it is hard for human beings to say what they feel and that we often have to search for the form of words before we can find the words themselves. Just as we, in our writing, have to find the words that fit what we are trying to express, the most appropriate words, so the characters in a story, novel or poem also have to discover the language that is fitting. Again, to learn to render this we have to listen to how people speak. How does a particular person begin? Does she dive straight to the point or does she circle around, feeling for what she wants to say? Does another person begin with 'Well, you know ...' or any other characteristic expression? In *John Thomas and Lady Jane*, Connie is distinguished from Parkin by the type of English she uses (middle class, standard). We can always tell who is speaking because they speak different languages.

If we listen acutely, we hear that everyone speaks a language that is in some way unique. Each person uses words in his or her own way; avoids some words, uses others frequently. We know this because sometimes we may use a word which we ourselves consider innocuous, only to find that it produces a strong emotional response in someone else. It carries a different meaning for them. Listening to the speech of those around us, we begin to discern how character reveals itself through words and also how people use words to veil themselves.

Conventions for writing dialogue

You may know what you want to write but remain unsure about the 'rules' for getting your dialogue onto the page. Let us look at three different ways of showing speech. We need to be aware that 'rules' (which are really just agreed-on conventions) are changing all the time, particularly since the line between inner voices and outer voices has become blurred.

Here is a passage from Kay Boyle's *Plagued by the Nightingale*:

> 'Come back, come back!' she shouted, but he pretended that he had not heard her at all.
>
> Down through the sea she splashed to him. If she held his hand, she thought, surely he could run faster with her than quite alone. Surely no tide could have them if they clasped hands and fled from it side by side.
>
> 'Nicolas, Nicolas, Nicolas,' she cried to him.
>
> 'Eh?' he said, lifting his head to her as if in irritation. 'What is it you want?'
>
> 'Come back, come back,' she shouted, 'the tide is coming in!'
>
> 'Well, what about it?' said Nicolas. She was coming close to him now.
>
> 'Give me your hand, Nicol,' she said. You must come back.'
>
> 'Why should I come back?' said Nicolas. He stood looking at her in his dark, gloomy way. 'What reason is there for me to go back?'
>
> She had grabbed his hand and his cane firmly in her hands and was trying to pull him back through the water.

This is the traditional and still most widely used way of making your characters speak. Everything Nicolas or Bridget says is wrapped in inverted commas, which open as the character opens his mouth and close as he closes it. Each speech is followed by 'she cried to him' or 'said Nicolas' to make it absolutely clear who's saying what.

You don't always need every 'he said' and 'she said'. They can be tedious if repeated too often – and if each character does have her own recognisable pattern of language, then the reader will know who is speaking without being told. If you removed all the 'he saids' and 'she saids' from the writing above you would still know who was saying what because Nicolas and Bridget are doing different things. Their actions distinguish them from one another. Bridget also calls Nicolas by his name more than once, which 'marks' him for the reader.

In a story from Cynthia Ozick's *Levitation*, the dialogue is made to move faster by leaving out the explanatory tail-pieces. Here is an argument between Mayor Puttermesser and Xanthippe, the golem with whose help the Mayor has gained political power:

> The Mayor upbraids Xanthippe: 'It's enough. I don't want him around here. Get rid of him.'
> Xanthippe writes: 'Jealousy!'
> 'I'm tired of hearing complaints from the cook. This is Gracie Mansion, it's not another kind of house.'
> 'Jealousy! He used to be yours.'
> 'You're stirring up scandal.'
> 'He brings me presents.'
> 'If you keep this up, you'll spoil everything.'
> 'My mother has purified the City.'
> 'Then don't foul it.'
> 'I am in contemplation of my future.'

Each character still begins a new line, so we know when a new person is speaking, but the 'said Puttermessers' and 'said Xanthippes' are pared to the bone: we have to deduce who is speaking from what they say and the way they say it. This affects the pace of the dialogue. It gives an impression of urgency, even breathlessness. We can tell that the writer is eager to take us to the climax. Dialogue of this type can be used effectively when the reader has settled into a story, knows exactly who's who by the way they speak, and is as anxious as the author to reach the crisis point. If it is used too early, it can be confusing so that the reader has to 'count back' to find out who is speaking and readers are not generally prepared to do that too often.

It is not crucial to start a new line each time a new person speaks, as long as the writer makes us *know* the speaker. John Betjeman bumps the speakers into one another in *Summoned By Bells*:

> 'I *love* Miss Usher,' Audrey said. 'Don't you?'
> 'Oh yes,' I answered. 'So do I' said Joc.

'We vote Miss Usher topping. Itchicoo!'
What was it I had done? Made too much noise?
Increased Miss Tunstall's headache? Disobeyed?
After Miss Usher had gone home to Frant,
Miss Tunstall took me quietly to the hedge:
'Now shall I tell you what Miss Usher said
About you, John?' 'Oh please, Miss Tunstall, do!'
'She said you were a common little boy.'

Three people talking are harder to handle than two, so Betjeman uses names more than Ozick. But Audrey, John and Joc are not facing one another in confrontation, as Puttermesser and Xanthippe are. They are three friends who have put their heads together to discuss the merits of a teacher, so they don't need the splendid isolation of a separate line each. Each speaker springs off from the one before, rather than opposes him. The form by which the dialogue is represented is the one that best fits the mood and subject of the dialogue. Notice, though, that when a particularly telling statement is being made ('We vote Miss Usher topping. Itchicoo!' and 'She said you were a common little boy.') it *does* have a line to itself. This is a way of drawing our attention and slowing us down so we concentrate more closely.

Inverted commas can even be abandoned in some cases. Look at this passage from James Joyce's *A Portrait of the Artist as a Young Man*:

> – Do you remember, he said, when we knew each other first? The first morning we met you asked me to show you the way to the matriculation class, putting a very strong stress on the first syllable. You remember? Then you used to address the jesuits as father, you remember? I ask myself about you: *Is he as innocent as his speech?*
>
> – I'm a simple person, said Davin. You know that. When you told me that night in Harcourt Street those things about your private life, honest to God, Stevie, I was not able to eat my dinner. I was quite bad. I was awake a long time that night. Why do you tell me those things?
>
> – Thanks, said Stephen. You mean I am a monster.
>
> – No, said Davin, but I wish you had not told me. A tide began to surge beneath the calm surface of Stephen's friendliness.
>
> – This race and this country and this life produced me, he said. I shall express myself as I am.

What does it mean to get rid of speech marks altogether? I think what is most evident is that the boundary line between what is spoken aloud and what is spoken inwardly, to oneself, becomes blurred. What Stephen says and what Stephen thinks begin to merge because the punctuation mark that indicates 'now my character speaks' is missing. Joyce does use the dash, however, to show that he is moving from descriptive narrative to direct expression. Does the dash have a different feel about it, different from the feel of speech marks? I think it does. To me it emphasises the speech more strongly, shows the characters *breaking into* speech rather than hanging up their speech marks to say 'Please, may I speak now?' Notice that Joyce doesn't even use speech marks for a speech within a speech, as where Stephen says: I ask myself about you: *Is he as innocent as his speech?* The words are italicised instead, which makes them stand out, as if starred by the new typeface.

We have now looked at four different ways of showing dialogue on the page and seen how each way is appropriate to the dialogue it represents. You may encounter other ways of showing speech, ways you can use in your own writing. You choose the form that best suits what you need to say, remembering always that the forms exist to help you say what you want to. They're not sacrosanct or eternal – even though, once you've chosen a form, it achieves its own custom of permanence. Once you start on a convention, you stay with it until the end of your story or poem.

What we say and what we write

To explore the differences between written dialogue and what people actually say to one another, we need to examine the relationship between the written word and other aspects of lived experience. In order to test out the connections between the two, try transcribing a conversation you've overheard on a bus, in a dentist's waiting room or round a meal table. You won't be able to catch all of it but get as much down as you can. It doesn't matter what the conversation is about: however inconsequential it seems, treat it as though all of it is important. Work at your transcription for four or five minutes. It's probably full of abbreviations and emendations because you've had to rush to get it all down, so take it home and write it up into recognisable dialogue.

Now look at it. What do you think of it? Does it interest you? Is it going anywhere? Do the characters reveal themselves through what they say? Your answers to these questions will begin to tell you how close you want your dialogue to come to the conversation you heard. If you thought what the people said possessed an intrinsic interest, if you wrote it down verbatim and pictured yourself as a sort of secretary to the outside world, recording something which had its own imaginative value but would otherwise have been lost, then you are one sort of writer – a naturalist. If, on the other hand, you judged the conversation you heard to be trivial and inconsequential and found yourself only selecting certain parts of it: if you changed it, rewrote it, rethought it completely so that it accorded with your own notion of how that conversation *should* have proceeded, then you are another sort of writer. You could be a realist, an expressionist or a *nouveau romancier* but the point is that you are not content to record things as they are. You believe that artistic expression involves some kind of radical transformation.

I myself think that the writer's relation to things as they are changes according to what he or she is writing. Sometimes we come very close to the world outside, for example when we hear someone say the words we need for a piece of writing we're involved in, we commit it lovingly to memory so we can use it. On the other hand, we sometimes withdraw completely from words as they are spoken, for example when we work on a dialogue that breaks certain social taboos, that shows characters saying things we cannot imagine people actually daring to say.

I want to recount an experience that has stayed with me ever since it happened, something that transformed an uneventful journey home from work. I think it illustrates the difference separating the writer's dialogue from the dialogue of everyday life.

One evening, tired, hungry and frazzled, I caught the tube home from central London. Anyone who has done this will know the feeling of being cramped in with other tired people, strap-hanging, sweating after a day at work. Conversation is almost non-existent. People don't have the energy to say much, preferring to use their newspapers to keep others at bay. From out of this irritated lassitude, a conversation began to reach me. When I looked up I saw it was coming from two smartly dressed men on the long bench-seat opposite. It went like this:

'Where are you off to over the weekend?'
'Oh, I thought we'd drive down to Stephanie's. She's just bought a little place down in Sussex. You know, fresh air, good food, wine, reading the Sunday newspapers out of reach of the telephone ...'

He went on at some length, with a slightly exaggerated middle-class accent, to enthuse over the pleasures of privileged country living. The man next to him smiled in total agreement. Then suddenly, the man on his other side, who was dressed as a hippy and had very long hair, said 'How boring!' The first man stopped in mid-flow and turned. 'I beg your pardon?' 'I said "How boring".' 'That's very impertinent of you. How do you know it's boring? I might think the things you do are boring. That book you're reading, for example, what is it?' 'Graham Green's *The Quiet American*.' 'Well, I know for a fact that Graham Greene is a very boring writer and that *The Quiet American* is his most boring book.'

By this time the whole tube carriage was riveted to the three men. It was delightful – not only to hear two of them boast so loudly about the lotus-eating weekend but to see what they said so effectively and hilariously challenged by a person from a different social group. I felt elated, and I think the other passengers did too, that the taboo against expressing oneself on the tube had been temporarily broken. The three men got off together, still avidly discussing Graham Greene. Everyone shifted around in their seats and relaxed. They all looked somehow looser. I certainly felt it had done me good and now whenever I recall it, I smile.

Afterwards I learned that the three men were actors, part of a company called The Theatre of the Tube. And when I thought back over the conversation, I realised that it was an extremely unlikely thing to have happened. Men don't usually conduct loud, enthusiastic duologues about rural delights (not English men, anyway) and it was even more unusual to hear someone butt in with 'Excuse me, I couldn't help overhearing, and what you're saying is absolute rubbish.' It was what I'd always wanted to happen but thought never would. When I say it like that I'm struck by how near that is to Pope's 'What e'er was thought/But ne'er so well expressed' definition of poetry. It seems to me that art of all kinds emerges out of deep human needs, needs that cannot be met anywhere else. That conversation would never have happened spontaneously. The three men might have thought those things but not have said them aloud. So the actors were speaking what would otherwise have remained unspoken.

Now look back at the extracts from Lawrence, Boyle, Ozick, Betjeman and Joyce. How much of that dialogue can you imagine actually being said? Can you imagine a shy working-class man (as Parkin is in *John Thomas and Lady Jane*) coming out with that lengthy, passionate declaration of love for Connie? I can't. I can imagine him saying 'Ah luv thee, but dunna ma'e me feel sma'' but it's hard for me to picture the careful explanation and vindication of himself that comes after. I think he *could* have said it but that he wouldn't have. That is to say, he could think through those ideas and feelings and in theory he could say them aloud but his shyness and his social position and the conventions about men expressing their feelings would have prevented him. That's if Parkin were a man in real life. But he's not, he's a character in a novel. In the novel I can believe he is saying such things, perhaps because I am hearing his voice in my head, in the privacy of my own mind (I am *thinking* him) and I am extremely relieved to hear him say them because his words bring to an end a certain kind of conflict between himself and Connie. The only way the conflict can ease is if Connie and Parkin communicate with one another. They may communicate more fully than they would in real life but this is to my advantage as the reader because it increases my relief and my pleasure. It allows me to savour the end of the conflict, to enjoy it in a way I could not have done if it had really happened, that is, if a few words had been exchanged, spoken with difficulty through the barbed-wire taboos that separate people in so-called intimate relationships. In the novel, Parkin's declaration leaves us in no doubt about what he feels and what he wants. Lawrence has given us something we could not easily get otherwise: he has given us *thought* spoken as *language*.

Look through the other extracts too. How much of the dialogue can you imagine being spoken in those circumstances? Nicolas and Bridget in *Plagued by the Nightingale* I can understand. It's the sort of 'You stupid boy, stop trying to drown yourself' speech I can imagine I would deliver if I were dragging a recalcitrant lad back to land. The Ozick extract is a particular case because it is a fantasy but it is the kind of clipped talk I think likely between two opponents who are squaring up to fight one another. The *Portrait of the Artist* extract is more difficult, in the same way I think the Lawrence extract is difficult. I can see Stephen and Davin thinking these things about one another but find it hard to imagine them expressing them aloud – if they existed as real people. But again, they don't, and Joyce is enabling us to hear something we could not hear outside his novel. The dialogues of both Joyce and Lawrence are performing what Eliot would call 'raids on the inarticulate'. They expand for us what we are able to think and say.

When Virginia Woolf first read Lawrence, she said she felt as if a curtain had been thrown back, so she could see, clearly, for the first time, the intensity of family relationships. That is what I take to be the goal of all writing: to open up fenced-off plots, to water tracts of land that have dried out, to make accessible thoughts and feelings that readers never knew they had or thought they were not allowed to have. In this sense writing, and particularly the writing of dialogue, performs a provocative, subversive and liberating role. It opens wider the realm of the possible.

Writing your own conflict

Rows between characters offer a superb opportunity for dialogue writing. Look at this passage from Ian McEwan's 'Psychopolis':

> At roughly the same time Terence said, 'Another objection to Christianity is that it leads to passive acceptance of social inequalities because the real rewards are in ...'
> And Mary cut across George in protest. 'Christianity has provided an ideology for sexism now, and capitalism ...'
> 'Are you a communist?' George demanded angrily, although I was not sure who he was talking to. Terence was pressing on loudly with his own speech. I heard him mention the Crusades and the Inquisition.
> 'More evil perpetrated in the name of Christ than ... this has nothing to do with ... to the persecution of women herbalists as witches ... Bullshit. It's irrelevant ... corruption, graft, propping up tyrants, accumulating wealth at the altars ... fertility goddess ... bullshit ... phallic worship ... look at Galileo ... this has nothing to ... ' I heard little else because now I was shouting my own piece about Christianity. It was impossible to stay quiet.

Notice how they are all so excited that they can no longer listen to one another. Four monologues begin at once, with the pace of the argument and the gaps in understanding between the four participants shown by the pregnant, rushing rows of dots. Remember this when you write an argument: that they depend, to a large extent, on the antagonists not hearing one another – for if they heard and understood one another, then a measure of sympathy would be extended and the continuance of the row would be threatened. All you need is an 'I know what you mean' or 'I can see what you're getting at' for an entirely different kind of discussion to begin. To maintain the row's high pitch of energy, you need to make sure that sympathy is withheld by all parties. This often entails making each character in some way deaf to what the others are saying.

Now imagine yourself once again in the room you love. You feel protected and at rest and you have a great desire for solitude. There is a knock at the door. It opens, without waiting for your 'Come in'. Suddenly, there facing you, is the person you least want to see at that moment. You may not dislike the person (or alternatively, you may) but you don't want to see him or her *then*, at all. You make it quite clear that you need to be alone, but the other person either cannot, or will not, hear. Your control breaks. A row ensues.

Write the whole incident.

5   Making a Short Story

What makes a short story? Characters, a setting, action of some kind, dialogue perhaps. These are the traditional ingredients but you will find stories that omit one or more of these to create a new effect or emphasis. You have worked on all these aspects of narrative in your exercises. If you mixed all your pieces of writing together, would they make a story? Or does a short story need something else, and if so, what is it?

I think it does. That 'something' could be the letter in the back of the drawer that nobody finds until it is too late. It is the unheard-of, something that only the author knows: the vital knowledge that gives the author control over both the characters and the readers of the book. You may object that I'm only describing the kind of action that occurs in whodunnit stories – but look again at the short fictions that have moved you. Can you say where the appeal lies? What is it about them that speaks to you, that calls forth such a strong response that at the end you feel satisfied, nourished, as though something new had taken place? It is crucial that you answer these questions for yourself, because through learning to understand the source of your own reading pleasure you will begin to see how to produce that pleasure for other readers.

T. S. Eliot aptly describes what happens in many short stories in 'The Love Song of J. Alfred Prufrock':

> Let us go, through certain half-deserted streets,
> The muttering retreats
> Of restless nights in one-night cheap hotels
> And sawdust restaurants with oyster-shells:
> Streets that follow like a tedious argument
> Of insidious intent
> To lead you to an overwhelming question …
> Oh, do not ask, 'What is it?'
> Let us go and make our visit.

A character will be led towards his own 'overwhelming question'. Some crisis, however small, will force a change in the fabric of his life and the author will understand and control this crisis, this change. Does the form of this story sound off echoes for you? Have you seen it before, in Maupassant's 'La Parure' ('The Necklace') or Henry James's 'The Beast in the Jungle'?

Take some time to *bathe* in short stories and look particularly at what the author is doing with the characters and the setting. In the two I've just mentioned you will find a character who lives many years without the benefit of some vital knowledge, something they really needed to know. Had they known it, their lives would have been completely different. The reader, too, labours on without this knowledge. It is revealed to the reader at the same time as the character. Too late. The character cannot benefit by what he or she now knows and all the reader can do is reflect on all that has been lost or missed. This is called *irony.*

> Irony *n., pl.* + **nies. 1.** the humorous or mildly sarcastic use of words to imply the opposite of what they normally mean. **2.** an instance of this, used to draw attention to some incongruity or irrationality. **3.** incongruity between what is expected to be and what actually is, or a situation or result showing such incongruity.
>
> Collins *English Dictionary*

In 'La Parure' and 'The Beast in the Jungle' the knowledge, which if the characters had possessed it would have changed their whole lives, is revealed right at the end. We can only imagine what they do with it. And really, because the story ends there, it doesn't matter what the characters do with it: the point is, what does *the reader* do with it? For it seems to me, that in this type of story, the author is teaching the reader a terrible lesson, is saying 'Look! This is what happens when a person lives locked inside a view of the world that does not take the existence of others into account.'

Another word for 'delusion' is 'mistake', 'fault' or 'flaw'. Maupassant's 'La Parure' tells the story of a woman who is bitterly dissatisfied with her lower middle-class, unexciting husband. She dreams of being adored, the centre of attention. When she and her husband have the chance to attend a ball, a rather grand function, she borrows an exquisite necklace from an acquaintance. They go to the ball, she is indeed admired by everyone there but when they get home she realises she has lost the necklace. She spends the next ten years taking in washing, slaving away to pay back the money they borrowed to replace it. At the end of this time, worn-down and aged far beyond her years, she meets the woman who lent her the necklace. The acquaintance is shocked, asks what could have happened to bring about this change, so the main character explains. At the end of the story, the lender admits 'It was paste' to the woman who has laboured for ten years. The fault or flaw here seems to lie in the woman's original dissatisfaction. The story leads us to ask questions like 'Why was she so displeased by her own life?', 'If she disliked it so much, why didn't she change it, instead of just dreaming of being adored?', 'Why didn't she value what she had?', 'Why didn't she buy a necklace she *knew* was paste, for the ball?'

We are witness to a disaster, a word which means 'a fault in the stars' (dis-aster). But since Cassius's 'The fault lies not in our stars, but in ourselves' we have found it hard to take external circumstances as the sole cause of terrible events. And because we are reading the story, we are at an imaginative level participating in the events, recognising aspects of ourselves in the main character. We see our own dissatisfactions, our own pointless, unfocused longings in her and we are forced, because we are shown the terrible thing that happens to her, to question aspects of ourselves which might otherwise remain unexamined. Four lines of T. S. Eliot's 'East Coker' come to mind here:

> The wounded surgeon plies the steel
> That questions the distempered part.
> Beneath the bleeding hands we feel
> The sharp compassion of the healer's art

The writer writes out of his own wounds and in doing so he enables his reader to experience emotional change, emotional growth, healing, without having to suffer the same fate as his character. In this type of short story, large claims are made about the effect of the reading experience. The underlying thrust is morality: the woman in 'La Parure' loses everything by her pointless longing. A delusion and a vain hope are opened up for us, so we can witness their terrible results. The author makes use of irony to point out a moral conclusion. We, the readers, are the only ones who can learn from the story: the characters have already lost everything.

Now try this out for yourself. Walk around the streets, looking carefully at people's faces. Wander aimlessly, taking your time. You will see a face that tells you something: there is a story in that face. Walk on and, during the course of half-an-hour's walk, imagine the secret the face reveals/conceals. Go home and write the story of the secret, divulging it to your reader at the very end. It is important that you *imagine* the secret, rather than steal it from a face you already know. When we write the stories of people we know, we often fall into the trap of identifying too strongly with our subject and not giving the reader enough to go on because the material is too familiar to us.

When I read out 'La Parure' to a writing class, I noticed that the penny dropped with some people just before the author disclosed the secret. Murmurs of 'It's paste' went around as I read the conversation between the two women. The reader *is* put into the position of detective in stories of this kind, so it's as well to remember that your story, too, will be combed for clues. Make sure that you tell your readers everything they need to know, so that when you deliver up your secret, they will greet it with absolute belief, with 'Of course. I should have guessed.'

Swallowing a glass of vodka

Not all short stories surprise the reader at the end. Some build up a sense of forboding that is either confirmed or denied, some make us laugh all the way through, some seem written only to outrage. It is hard to find a common thread. Perhaps we need to look not at their content or form, but at their effect when we try to ascertain what is true for all of them – at least, all the stories that *work*. Anton Chekhov said that reading a short story 'feels rather like swallowing a glass of vodka'. Does that seem right to you? A quick, sharp beverage that hits you in the throat and then in the guts; that changes, perhaps only for a time, your way of seeing the world? A novel would be different: a source of sustenance over days or weeks, something to keep you going. There may be surprises, but they are woven into the fabric, the kinds of surprises you live with. In the short story there doesn't seem to be that kind of time for the characters to digest and integrate the surprise into their lives. They experience it and they are gone. The task of integration is left to the reader.

So what *is* a story? A piece of writing where something happens? Or where nothing happens? (Montaigne said that 'even constancy is a more sluggish form of movement'.) Where something is seen to change? But how do we show change? By showing things as they are, then showing them penetrated by the catalyst, the agent that embodies the will to change.

What is your earliest memory of a story where something or somebody changed? Because our conscious memories are selective, because we remember stories that meant something to us, that *spoke* to us, your answer will reveal to you a great deal about the way you used stories when you were a child.

Until recent years, when the popularity of the short story has greatly increased, it was looked upon as a sort of poor relation to the novel, something the novelist did to occupy idle time, rather like whittling wood. But if we include children's literature in our survey, then the short story occupies a more permanently important place. Our first introduction to the world of the imagination is made in fairy tales, folk tales, shaggy dog stories, elaborately told jokes and the dramatic scenarios we invent for ourselves, our friends and our toys.

Psychologists believe that we hold on to certain stories because they enable us to make sense of an otherwise confusing world – that we learn through stories and see our way through to maturity with their help:

> In early adolescence a girl had been fascinated by 'Hansel and Gretel', and had derived great comfort from reading and re-reading it, fantasizing about it. As a child, she had been dominated by a slightly older brother. He had, in a way, shown her the path, as Hansel did when he put down the pebbles which guided his sister and himself back home. As an adolescent, this girl continued to rely on her brother, and this feature of the story felt reassuring. But at the same time she also resented the brother's dominance. Without her being conscious of it at the time, her struggle for independence rotated around the figure of Hansel. The story told her unconscious that to follow Hansel's lead led her back, not forward, and it was also meaningful that although Hansel was the leader at the story's beginning, it was Gretel who in the end achieved freedom and independence for both, because it was she who defeated the witch. As an adult, this woman came to understand that the fairy tale had helped her greatly in throwing off her dependence on her brother, as it had convinced her that an early dependence on him need not interfere with her later ascendancy. Thus, a story which for one reason had been meaningful to her as a young child provided guidance for her at adolescence for quite a different reason.
>
> Bruno Bettelheim, *The Uses of Enchantment*

Think back to all the stories that affected you strongly as a child. Can you remember which part exerted the special emotional pull, the part that brought you back to the story again and again? And what about the part the stories played in your emotional development? If you love a story, you know it all the way through. Did you, like the girl Bettelheim speaks of, dwell on different stages at different times, according to your need? When we include fairy stories in our consideration of 'the short story', we realise how central they have been to our childhood, adolescence and adulthood, too: how we have pored eagerly over them because we ourselves, like Snow White, have feared our mother's envy; because, like Little Briar Rose, we imagine the gap between the child and the woman to stretch over a hundred years; because, like Cinderella, we long to be protected by the good mother from the bad mother. Seen in this way, it is clear that fairy tales play a significant part in helping us grow up – and that they are able to do this because they introduce us to ideas about change, conflict and coming to maturity through the medium of make-believe. A thread that runs through all fairy tales, and is important for our own writing, is the element of change. A world which is wrong, which contains envy and malice, is reordered, made new. The hero or heroine is helped to overcome the destructive aspects of her world and becomes part of a richer, more integrated whole.

If you look through all the short stories you know, I think you'll find that the element of change lies at the bottom of each, like an insistent bass line. Something always happens and someone always has to deal with (or avoid) what has occurred. The character can meet the change head on, in which case we may feel gratified – or sidestep the new knowledge, try to behave as though everything is the same as before. Either way, the change *sits* there for the reader, fascinating, not to be ignored. Sometimes the most immense changes are given to us in a short story of only a few pages: Chekhov's 'Let Me Sleep' sees an exhausted, brutalised servant-girl murder a baby in six pages; Katherine Mansfield's 'Revelations' sees a woman who longs for freedom and independence rush for security to an unloved but ardent suitor – because everything feels strange at her hairdresser's, where she learns that a tragedy has occurred – in seven pages.

You may object: 'But changes happen in novels, too. Even in poems. Certainly in plays.' Yes, but in the short story, everything is subordinate to the change. It is the change that counts, rather than the characters or the setting. These elements, much more central to

the novel, interlock with the transformation, feed into it, determine it
even, but they do not overshadow it. Edith Wharton called a volume
of her short stories *Crucial Instances* and that is a good way of
describing the form. The short story shows us a character at a crucial
instant in her life (parallels with the fairy tale emerge here) and traces
the effect of that instant upon her.

Your method of narration is likely to be different in a short story.
You haven't the time for lengthy character analysis or exquisite evoca-
tions of place. These must be done with swift strokes, as if you were
drawing a cartoon rather than painting in oil. Imagine your main
character. What are the four most significant aspects of his being?
Imagine your place. What makes it unique? Why does the change
have to happen there? It is the difference between what Jean Piaget
calls 'syncretistic and analytic vision'. Syncretistic vision represents
the salient visible details, the hero's Brylcreemed hair and pocketful
of peanuts, rather than seeking to explain him in terms of his social
and intellectual background. The short story writer will find ways of
giving the character by concentrating on details of dress, facial
expression, speech and action, leaving the reader to fill in the picture
for her or himself. If the outline is firm, the reader will do the rest of
the work.

Making changes

Imagine the scenarios for four short stories. You may not wish to write
them all but imagine them nevertheless and draft out the pattern of
the story. Four changes: the crucial details for each. In this exercise
you will prove to yourself that you can invent something quite new, a
change which perhaps connects with your own life but is seen from
the outside, happening to someone else.

Before you begin, look at the way Katherine Mansfield sketched the
outlines for her last stories:

STORIES FOR MY NEW BOOK

N.Z. *Honesty:* The Doctor, Arnold Cullen and his wife Lydia, and Archie
the friend.
L. *Second Violin:* Alexander and his friend in the train. Spring ... wet
lilac ... spouting rain.

N.Z. *Six Years After:* A wife and husband on board a steamer. They see someone who reminds them. The cold buttons.

L. *Lives Like Logs of Driftwood:* This wants to be a long, very well written story. The men are important, especially the lesser man. It wants a great deal of working ... newspaper office.

N.Z. *A Weak Heart:* Roddie on his bike in the evening, with his hands in his pockets, *doing marvels* by that dark tree at the corner of May Street.

L. *Widowed:* Geraldine and Jimmie, a house overlooking Sloane Street and Square. Wearing those buds at her breast. 'Married or not married' ... From autumn to spring.

(L. and N.Z. refer to London and New Zealand, the settings for the stories.)

Katherine Mansfield, *The Collected Short Stories*

Mansfield thought out her stories first, made brief notes to remind herself of the details, of the change that was to take place, and *then* wrote. She wrote in her journal on New Year's Day 1922:

Wrote *The Doves' Nest* this afternoon. I was in no mood to write; it seemed impossible. Yet, when I had finished three pages, they 'were all right!' This is a proof (never to be too often proved) that when one has thought out a story nothing remains but the *labour.*

There are at least two schools of thought on the way short stories come to be written. One holds that the writer does most of the work beforehand, laying a plan that is rather like an egg – and the story hatches, almost of its own accord. The other holds that we discover what we have to say through the process of writing – D.H. Lawrence would support this view. There may be a middle road, too: one that knows the importance of the preliminary schema but is not surprised if something new emerges in the actual writing. If you believe, as I do, that miracles sometimes take place between the brain and the writing hand, that we do not always know what we want to write until we have written it, then you will be gratified when the unconscious makes one of its surprising and glorious forays onto the page, and not seek to suppress what has been given without your asking.

6 Speaking in Different Tongues, Different Tones

We have concentrated up to now on ways of starting to write in our own voice: through calling up early memories, waking up the senses and developing an ear for the rhythms of speech. But what if you have more than one writing voice? (You have.) What if there are several voices inside you, all waiting to be heard? (There are.) If you think about your own personality, you will recognise that even your conscious self is composed of different facets. With one friend you may be the epitome of patient listening, with another the garrulous fool. With a lover you may be tender, or outrageously jealous, and with a child you may be alternately nurturing, supportive and strict, even punitive. Each one of us is many people. Just think of all the people you are at different times, in different places. Think of all the selves you put on – selves that aren't really masks because they are a true part of the core being – but that often coexist uneasily, compelling us to recognise the tension and contradictions between the different selves. If we feel whole, then all these aspects of our being seem to be looped together in a loose, flexible unity. The contradictions remain but they only become tension and conflict when we are under pressure to perform more than one role at a time.

Writers, as I've argued before, tend to use these contradictions rather than try to pretend they're not there. Being a writer is in itself a type of contradiction because it means that you are both an actor, a participant in the world, and also an observer, an interpreter, a maker of meaning. In this chapter we will channel our energies into opening up the contradictory facets of our personalities and explore the different voices, different tones of voice, that these contradictions make available to us. The two voices I want us to concentrate on are 'the laughing voice' and 'the Gothic voice'.

The laughing voice

First we have to consider carefully what makes us laugh. Examine all the humour you come across – in shops, at work, with children, on the TV – and try to ascertain what it is that makes something funny for you. You will find the apparently mechanical task of taking jokes and funny situations apart, to see what elements they're composed of, extremely helpful for your own work. Perhaps you're saying 'I can't do that. Cutting it up like a load of old fish.' Don't be afraid of doing this. We don't destroy humour just because we seek to understand it. And we need to understand it so we can produce it ourselves.

Trevor Griffiths asks many painful, searching questions about laughter and humour in his play *The Comedians*. In the unlikely setting of an adult education evening class for would-be comics, a once-famous comedian puts forward his views about what comedy should do. He believes it should take the parts of our lives that are most sore, most hurtful, most unspoken, most taboo and bring them into the public sphere. When these deeply hidden parts of ourselves are spoken out, they produce a feeling of relief in the audience because they have similar wounds, similar fears and that relief often comes out as laughter. Like the Jewish American comedian Joan Rivers, for example, who tells jokes about herself as a Jewish woman that key into other women's silent insecurities. When she was interviewed on the television recently she said things like:

> *Interviewer:* I understand your husband had a heart attack recently.
> *Joan Rivers:* Yes. Thankfully, he's getting better now. But I gave it to him you know. We were making love, and I took the paper bag off my head.
> *Interviewer:* You have very strong views on women in bed.
> *Joan Rivers:* Yes. To start with, a woman must fake in bed, must fake orgasm. It's common courtesy.
> *Interviewer:* You say you're not happy about your body.
> *Joan Rivers:* Hell no. My thighs are so wobbly. Thank God my stomach covers them. I said to my husband the other day 'Say something nice to me. Say something nice about my legs.' He said 'Blue goes with everything.'

In simply giving voice to the fears of ageing that our society makes sure women have, Joan Rivers has discovered a rich vein of comedy.

And in turning the fear into laughter by speaking it out, she is participating in one of comedy's most valuable functions: that of disrupting
the status quo. If we can laugh out loud about getting old, break the
silence that surrounds it instead of suffering quietly, then we are
beginning to escape from a fear society wants us to have – so we will
buy uplift bras, expensive face creams and continue to fear and envy
younger women. By speaking out about envy between women,
comedy can play a part in helping us to heal it in ourselves.

In *The Comedians*, when the once-famous comic tries to explain the
healing power of humour, he has to work against his students, who
keep falling back into racist, sexist jokes, jokes about cripples, jokes
about anyone who is different. They tell these jokes when they get
nervous, because they are easy, always sure to get a laugh. This is the
humour that does not heal, the sort that encourages hatred of out-
siders. It is the pantomime humour we all grew up with, where the
compere talks about the organist's big organ and his steamed up
glasses. Fundamentally, it is about embarrassment and shame and
keeping us all in our place.

When you consider what makes you laugh, try to distinguish
between the humour that opens things up, that enables you to confront painful areas and makes you feel stronger, and the humour that
operates at the level of the stock response, works on your fear, keeps
your defences up and makes you feel weaker. The two types of
humour perform opposing functions, pull in opposite directions. The
first type can help to produce writing of lasting benefit, while the
second does nothing but increase fear and prejudice.

Here is a passage from *The Secret Diary of Adrian Mole*. If it makes
you laugh, try to discover where the pleasure comes from:

Sunday April 5th
PASSION SUNDAY

Nigel came round this morning. He is still mad about Pandora. I tried to
take his mind off her by talking about the Norwegian leather industry
but he couldn't get interested somehow.

I made my father get up at 1 p.m. I don't see why he should lie stink-
ing in bed all day when I am up and about. He got up and went outside
to clean the car. He found one of my mother's earrings down the side of
the back seat and he just sat there staring at it. He said 'Adrian, do you
miss your mother?' I replied, 'Of course I do, but life must go on.' He
then said, 'I don't see why.' I took this to mean that he was suicidal, so I

immediately went upstairs and removed anything harmful from the bathroom.

After we had eaten our frozen roast-beef dinner and I was washing up, he shouted from the bathroom for his razor. I lied and shouted back that I didn't know where it was. I then removed every knife and sharp instrument from the kitchen drawer. He tried to get his battery razor to work but the batteries had leaked and gone all green.

I like to think I am broad-minded, but the language my father used was beyond the pale, and all because he couldn't have a shave! Tea was a bit of a drag. My grandma kept saying horrible things about my mother and my father kept rambling on about how much he missed her. Nobody even noticed I was in the room! The dog got more attention than me!

My grandma told my father off for growing a beard. She said 'You may think it amusing to look like a communist, George, but I don't.' She said that even in the trenches at Ypres my grandad had shaved every day. Sometimes he had to stop rats from eating his shaving soap. She said that my grandad was even shaved by the undertaker when lying in his coffin, so if the dead could shave there was no excuse for the living. My father tried to explain, but grandma didn't stop talking once so it was a bit difficult.

We were both glad when she went home.

Looked at *Big and Bouncy*. It is Passion Sunday after all!

I think that here, Sue Townsend is playing with notions of expected behaviour. Adrian Mole says and does things we would not expect from an adolescent. He is up and about before his father and he gets his father up, as if *he* were the parent and his father the sleepy child. We don't expect Adrian to say 'life must go on'. He is stoical and resigned, while his father is emotional. Adrian becomes the over-protective parent to his miserable father and although we can understand how this behaviour comes about in a child whose parents are asserting their own needs, who are themselves needy children, it nevertheless feels funny, feels inappropriate. He is a child aping the conventional responses of an adult. He takes care of his parents because they can no longer take care of him or themselves. Perhaps this accounts for our dual response to the book: we are simultaneously moved to tears *and* laughter.

There is also a tendency to state the obvious in a way that stops it from being obvious. When Adrian writes 'Nobody even noticed I was in the room!' with its exclamation mark of outrage at the end, part of us says 'Of course they didn't notice. They were too busy arguing about your mother to see you,' while another part understands and sides with Adrian's outrage: 'There's no of course about it. How *could* they ignore you?' The author undermines 'adult' notions of what is normal and natural and obvious by showing them through the eyes of a young boy who is trying to puzzle it all out.

Sue Townsend has an eye and an ear for the ridiculous: the thought of a son putting away all sharp instruments to stop his father killing himself moves us to laughter. And the grandmother's homily, in all its macabre detail, leading up to 'so if the dead could shave there's no excuse for the living', releases a humorous response because it seems just what a respectable parent *would* say, in desperation to whip her errant son back to the straight and narrow. We recognise the ridiculous details because they are also a part of our own lives.

I recently heard Alan Bennett talking about the humour in his plays and he said that he began to develop his ear for the ridiculous simply by listening to members of his family. He remembered sitting in silence with his grandmother as evening drew on ('always in darkness because she had the idea that light was expensive') while she occasionally read out a headline from the newspaper. The darkness would be pierced by statements like 'Pope braves drizzle' and 'I see the president of Romania's mother's dead. There's allers trouble for somebody.' I am not sure why the idea of an old woman in an unlit room reading out newspaper headlines for her grandson tickles me so, but it does. I think part of it has to do with recognition – I remember listening to my own grandmother's mysterious pronouncements – and part with a renewed sense of the strangeness of it. There is a connection with Joan Rivers here. If she hadn't spoken those secret fears ('I am so ugly. I will surely give someone a heart attack. I have varicose veins in my legs. I must cover them up.') they would remain unexamined, unchallenged. By hearing them, we recognise them and we also, perhaps for the first time, see them as strange. We hear her speak, we hear the other women laughing and we think 'If we all have these fears, why need we be afraid? I am no uglier than anyone else. My ugliness is becoming strange to me.'

The Gothic voice

Our other voice, the Gothic voice, can give us a very different sensation. Comedy can give comfort and security, can make us feel more at home in our skin. Gothic horror does the opposite: it frightens us out of our skin, discomforts us and turns what we think we know into something unreal and daunting. Whereas comedy can enable us to know the world better, stories of mystery and horror insist on all we cannot know and therefore increase our fear of a disordered, malefic universe. Gothic tales are characterised by gloom, the grotesque and the supernatural. In a peculiar way, Gothic tales are related to comedy. They both show us a topsy-turvy world, a world turned inside-out by the particular lens through which it is viewed. But whereas comedy is capable of taking us out of fear, the Gothic tends to take us further in.

Let's begin by naming our own fears. Which of the following frighten you?

birds	being pursued
cats	knowing that someone knows your secret
rats	blood
dead bodies	the dark
locked rooms	open spaces
thick curtains	strangers
being watched	strange-looking people
being alone	being taken over by someone else
being locked in	what else?

If you're at all like me, your list will be very long. Sometimes, just thinking about fear is enough to start the palms sweating. It would seem that our capacity to feel fear is great and the merest trigger can set it off. So what makes us want to read stories that frighten us? The psychotherapist says 'Look at the wish behind the fear.' Look at the wish to be locked in, the wish for the dark, the wish to be watched, to have one's secrets known, to be taken over by someone else. And look at the way the wish connects with the fear, in a kind of fascinated ambivalence, a horrified curiosity about experiencing, through litera-ture, something we may unconsciously want but by which we are consciously appalled.

When was the first time you were in the dark, locked in and taken over by someone else? Think back, into the dark, the dark places, the place even before conscious memory. The place you had to fight your way out of, shouting and wailing as you first hit the light; the place that imprisoned you, yet kept you warm, fed you. The place where you were not yourself, but an appendage, a parasite on someone else. Think back to the time before you were you. It is impossible with our conscious mind to fully know what we feel about this place but the Gothic tale can set in motion atavistic fears and fantasies. An atavism is a throwback, a 'primitive' reaction (it literally means 'great-grand-father's grandfather') – something the writer must know about in himself if his work is to resonate in his readers.

In 'The Fall of the House of Usher', Edgar Allan Poe invokes the fear of being shut in which he projects into the fear of shutting someone else in. In this case, Madeline Usher has been buried in the family vault below the house, supposedly dead:

> It was, especially, upon retiring to bed late in the night of the seventh or eighth day after the placing of the Lady Madeline within the donjon, that I experienced the full power of such feelings. Sleep came not near my couch – while the hours waned and waned away. I struggled to reason off the nervousness which had dominion over me. I endeav-oured to believe that much, if not all of what I felt, was due to the bewil-dering influence of the gloomy furniture in the room – of the dark and tattered draperies, which, tortured into motion by the breath of a rising tempest, swayed fitfully to and fro upon the walls, and rustled uneasily about the decorations of the bed. But my efforts were fruitless. An irre-pressible tremor gradually pervaded my frame; and, at length, there sat upon my very heart an incubus of causeless alarm. Shaking this off with a gasp and a struggle, I uplifted myself upon the pillows, and, peering earnestly within the intense darkness of the chamber, hearkened – I know not why, except that an instinctive spirit prompted me – to certain low and indefinite sounds which came, through the pauses of the storm, at long intervals, I knew not whence. Overpowered by an intense sentiment of horror, unaccountable yet unendurable, I threw on my clothes with haste (for I felt that I should sleep no more during the night), and endeavoured to arouse myself from the pitiable condi-tion into which I had fallen, by pacing rapidly to and fro through the apartment.

When we look at Poe's tales, the structure seems predictable, even for-mulaic: the dawning sense that all is not as it should be; the attempts to explain away the moaning sounds that something inside him is nev-ertheless compelling him to hear; the fight with fancy, as if one could will away one's deepest fear; and then the horrified recognition that what one was most afraid of is *there*, behind the antique panels, waiting to throw one to the floor. But if all this forms part of a familiar pattern, why are we still afraid when we read it? Perhaps it is because, although we can consciously trace the outline of the fear, it reaches so far into the hidden recesses of our minds that we cannot control the involuntary response. Perhaps it speaks to a part of our mind that does not know about self-control – a part that remembers the time when we were entirely in someone else's power and he or she, in a certain sense, were in ours.

Poe calls up all these feelings – and leaves us stranded on their shores. One has the sense that he himself was beached there and that one of his comforts lay in writing out his fears in order to bring his readers to the same sands where he lay struggling for air. Poe does not seem to know his way back into the water.

There are stories, however, that *know* the depths of these fears, take their readers into them, into the experience, and then out through the other side. These are the stories that possess the gift of healing. The reader feels, after reading them, as if he/she had followed Theseus into the labyrinth, faced the Minatour and helped to slay the beast, then followed the clew back into the outside world. The reader assists at the triumph over the abyss and experiences, in a very important way, his/her own coming-through or rite of passage. I have said that Poe's tales take the reader to somewhere he/she is not him or herself; these Gothic stories *restore* the reader to him or herself.

One Gothic tale I am thinking of in particular is the Grimm's fairy tale called 'Fitcher's Bird', which is the prototype for all the Bluebeard stories. In it, a wizard enchants two sisters, one after the other, to accompany him to his house in the depth of the forest. They each fall utterly under his spell and promise to obey him in everything, whereupon he tells them that he has to go on a journey and gives them the keys of his magnificent house but forbids them to enter a room which is opened by a particular little key. He also gives each of them an egg to take care of. The first, then the second, sister is overcome by curiosity and enters the bloody chamber:

> A great bloody basin stood in the middle of the room, and hard by was a block of wood, and a gleaming axe lay upon it. She was so terribly alarmed that the egg which she held in her hand fell into the basin. She got it out and wiped the blood off, but in vain; it appeared again in a moment. She washed and scrubbed, but she could not get it off.

When the wizard returns he punishes each sister for her curiosity:

> He threw her down, dragged her along by her hair, cut her head off on
> the block, and hewed her in pieces. Then he threw her into the basin ...
>   Then he went and brought the third sister, but she was clever and
> wily. When he had given her the keys and the egg, and had left her, she
> first put the egg away with great care, and then examined the house,
> and at last went into the forbidden room. Alas, what did she behold!
> Both her dear sisters lay there in the basin, cruelly murdered, and cut in
> pieces. But she began to gather their limbs together and put them in
> order, head, body, arms and legs. And when nothing further was
> wanting the limbs began to move and unite themselves together, and
> both the maidens opened their eyes and were once more alive. Then
> they rejoiced and kissed and caressed each other.

The third sister then puts into operation an elaborate plan to get all
the wizard's gold and trap him and all his cohorts in his house, to
which her brothers then set fire. She vanquishes the wizard by
keeping her wits, by resisting his enchantment. She is just as curious
as her sisters, but she has the foresight to put the egg safely away
before penetrating the forbidden chamber.

Look at the fears/wishes that are called up in 'Fitcher's Bird': the
fear of being enchanted, of having one's own will overcome by that of
another; the fear of being punished for one's curiosity, one's will-to-
know; the fear of being locked forever in the bloody chamber. They
hook into our own deepest fantasies. *We* are the wizard's victim, too.

In this way the story is just like one of Poe's: it calls up buried fears.
It also calls upon the symbols most likely to draw us in – an egg, keys,
blood and gold. These things mean something different to each one of
us but they are central to the culture as a whole and central to our
knowledge and fantasies about our own bodies. They seem almost
magical in themselves and once incorporated in a story they are guaranteed to weave a web to catch and hold us.

I think one of the reasons 'Fitcher's Bird' is at once so fascinating
and so satisfying is that the third sister is not protected from the
enchantment. She is just as much under the wizard's spell as the ones
who have gone before; her curiosity is as great. She is just cleverer.
Her wits, her power to organise the symbols (to put the egg away and
put the bodies back together) ensure her final victory. She can use the
enchantment, rather than be overcome by it, because a critical, rational, intelligent, witty part of herself retains its distance. In a way

she is a model for the writer in you – the writer who needs to experience the passion, the enchantment, yet keep enough control to effectively organise your symbols. You cannot be completely enchanted yourself because it is your job to enchant others. You are the lover who will woo your readers, who will bring them under your power by the words you write.

Now you need to bring a friend or friends in to help you with your writing because it is time now to test out its effect upon other people:

1. Take one or more of the elements of humour you discovered in yourself and use them to write a funny story. Remember the connection between humour and pain and humour and the taboo. Don't be afraid to open up uncharted areas or kick down a few fences. Your task is to write a gift of laughter for your friend.

2. Take your biggest fear, take three or four symbols (for example, a door, an attic, a ring, a knife) that hold significance for you and organise a story around the fear and the symbols. When you consider this organisation, bear in mind Poe's description of the short story as 'a narrative that can be read at one sitting of from half an hour to two hours, that is limited to a certain unique and single effect *to which every detail is subordinate.*' Give it to a friend to read and find out what effect it had.

7 Hold the Tension, Hold the Energy

So far we have concentrated on taking control of feelings of humour or fright so you can represent them in a way which will evoke strong feelings in your readers. Now we need to explore how to sustain the states of mind you call up.

Sometimes I find that stories and poems lose force and energy half-way through. A tremendous amount of care and ardour has gone into the beginning and then the story tails off, almost as if that initial effort had been too much. This might happen because the writer is tired, because he or she wants to get the writing over and done with; but the fundamental reason seems to be that the writer has broken contact with the feeling that originally made him or her want to write the story or poem. If that contact is broken, the words and events become a sort of empty recitation, an alienated recounting of something that cannot proclaim its real significance. The gap between words and experience is already great; at its best, the language struggles towards a fullness it can never achieve. We often hear people say 'I can't express how I felt' or 'Words are inadequate.' These sayings aren't just conscious evasions. Words are always inadequate. But some get closer to the feeling, the experience or the thought than others. And the writer has to keep conjuring the feeling in him or herself, to keep it *there*, if he/she is to hope to do the same for the readers. In this chapter we shall work on ways of maintaining the connection with the feeling that animates, gives life to the story or the poem.

Let's begin by looking at a well-known poem – William Blake's 'London'. I believe it is the most powerful poem he ever wrote and I want to analyse the way in which he maintains the clenched fist of resistant energy through four rhyming quatrains:

London

I wander through each charter'd street,
Near where the charter'd Thames does flow,

And mark in every face I meet
Marks of weakness, marks of woe.

In every cry of every Man,
In every Infant's cry of fear,
In every voice, in every ban,
The mind-forg'd manacles I hear.

How the Chimney-sweeper's cry
Every black'ning Church appalls;
And the hapless Soldier's sigh
Runs in blood down Palace Walls.

But most through midnight streets I hear
How the youthful Harlot's curse
Blasts the new born Infant's tear,
And blights with plagues the Marriage hearse.

Think first about the repetitions Blake uses: 'charter'd' occurs twice in the first stanza, and 'marks' three times. Why are these words repeated? What part does repetition play in creating a mood of sorrow, of hopelessness? Sometimes, when writing, we repeat a word unknowingly and when we read it again we recognise that our pen has slipped back over old ground: we have not found the right word. But here something different is happening. It is as if Blake is taking our hand and compelling us to see what he sees: streets mapped out, chartered, known, possessing no vital life of their own but *owned*; a river that has been forced to fit into this scheme, that is likewise owned, and hence deprived of some intrinsic quality that should belong to rivers. Faces are marked – stained or branded, disfigured. Repeating these words leads the reader to think that the poet sees these things everywhere he looks.

Look at the rhythm of the poem:

I wander through each charter'd street

– di *dum* di *dum* di *dum* di *dum*. It is one of the commonest rhythms to be found but look what it does here. It is the limping walk of someone who has been crippled – the Greek name for it is the 'iamb', which means 'lame man' – people who have been *manacled, marked, banned, chartered*. Not only does the rhythm fit with what the poet is saying, it plays its own central part in creating the mood and meaning of the poem.

In the first stanza, the poet tells us what he sees; in the second, what he hears. Blake is using one sense after the other, as you have learnt to do. By doing this, he is able to show different sides of a thought or feeling, building up the sense impressions that cluster around it. He could have written, 'Every time I walk through London I realise how chained down everybody is, how people make one another suffer, how no one is free from corruption' – and he would have been greeted with our 'Yes, so you think that. So what?' It has no emotional effect upon the reader because it doesn't show how the poet came to these conclusions. And as the aim of a writer is to take the reader with him, we can learn from the way Blake leads us along the path he is taking.

Look at the connections Blake makes in the third and fourth stanzas. The chimney sweep is bound to the church, not only because he cleans the chimneys that pump out the soot that disfigures the church but also because the church preaches a kind of Christianity that can countenance beating, starving and insanely cruel treatment towards chimney sweeps. Soldiers are compelled to fight, to bleed, to die, to safeguard the interest of the crown and the state – and Blake makes a metaphor out of that connection by having the soldier's sigh run *in blood* down the walls of the palace.

These connections open out – inevitably, it seems – into the most terrible bond, in the fourth stanza: that between the 'holy', respectable institution of marriage and the harsh, exploitative world of prostitution, where bodies are bought and sold. In the last two stanzas, Blake is explaining the *marks of woe* that he sees in the first stanza – but what extraordinary connections to make! Outrageous they seem at first. Surely it is a kind of blasphemy to hold the church responsible for the cruelty and degradation going on around its blackened doors? Surely it is treacherous to blame the palaces of the rich for all the blood spilt on battle-fields? Surely marriage and prostitution are separate and it insults marriage to imply that they thrive on one another? These are the astonished questions we ask when we first read the poem. But when the dust has settled, when we consider what we know – from reading history, from films, from our own experience – we realise that although it *is* outrageous, the connections Blake makes are true ones.

Try to remember the things you've learnt from this poem until you do the next exercise when you will have the opportunity to transform the knowledge into something uniquely your own. In the *writer's* place in your mind, retain these key words:

- repetitions
- rhythm
- sense impressions
- new connections

until it is time to do something with them. If you do this, you will be making your first experiment with Hemingway's 'letting the well fill up again' before you return to write. Hemingway claimed that he always stopped writing about noon, when he knew what was coming next. He then forced himself to get through the rest of the day without writing, so that the well would have replenished its juice by the time he took up his pencil again the next daybreak.

It is to Hemingway's writing I now want us to turn, to a piece of reportage published in 1935 called 'Who murdered the Vets?' The Vets in question are war veterans stationed along the Florida Keys, employed by the United States government to build a railway track. They are, Hemingway writes, 'doing coolie labor for a top wage of $45 a month and they have been put down on the Florida Keys where they can't make trouble. It is hurricane months, sure, but if anything comes up, you can always evacuate them, can't you?' The Vets were not evacuated when the hurricane struck and Hemingway reports on the wind and the tidal wave that killed hundreds of them. What I find fascinating about these eight pages is that they are sustained by rage – by a controlled yet immense rage against a government which could allow its veterans to die – and that Hemingway has the skill to let his anger unroll, rather like one of the giant waves caused by the hurricane, until his readers are held afloat upon it. It is this rage which draws us in, which has us participating in Hemingway's feelings before we know it, that makes the piece so powerful. We need to learn and understand how he *composes* his rage, so we can harness similar potencies in our own writing.

The piece begins in an unlikely way – with three direct accusations:

> Whom did they annoy and to whom was their possible presence a political danger?
> Who sent them down to the Florida Keys and left them there in hurricane months?
> Who is responsible for their deaths?

Hemingway seems to have 'gone off on top doh' and fired all his big guns before the battle has even begun. But after this opening blast, in which he makes clear the depth of his anger, the tone is immediately reined in, measured. 'The writer of this article lives a long way from Washington and would not know the answers to these questions.' That itself is something we can take in: his way of surprising the reader, setting up a kind of emotional ambush, by a sudden switch from violent to measured tone. Hemingway takes us through a hurricane which is predicted, which comes very near but finally misses his home. In doing this, he takes us over the ground first, telling us what to expect, what to look for, so that when the hurricane does hit, it hits us harder:

> When we reached Lower Matecumbe there were bodies floating in the ferry slip. The brush was all brown as though autumn had come to these islands where there is no autumn but only a more dangerous summer, but that was because the leaves had all been blown away. There was two feet of sand over the highest part of the island where the wind had carried it and all the heavy bridge-building machines were on their sides. The island looked like the abandoned bed of a river where the sea had swept it. The railroad embankment was gone and the men who had cowered behind it and finally, when the water came, clung to the rails, were all gone with it. You could find them face down and face up in the mangroves. The biggest bunch of the dead were in the tangled, always green but now brown, mangroves behind the tank cars and the water towers. They hung on there, in shelter, until the wind and rising water carried them away. They didn't all let go at once but only when they could hold on no longer. Then further on you found them high in the trees where the water had swept them. You found them everywhere and in the sun all of them were beginning to be too big for their blue jeans and jackets that they could never fill when they were on the bum and hungry.

By this time we feel as if we are Hemingway's companion, hauling out the bodies one by one, so that when he says 'Well you waited a long time to get sick brother. Sixty-seven of them and you get sick at the sixty-eighth', it is as if he is saying it to us over his shoulder as he bends down to examine another body. He is talking directly to us and we *do* feel sick.

What do we learn from this piece of reportage? That we can, must, involve the reader, make the reader participate in the feeling we are trying to represent; and we learn, too, that there are some subjects, like this one, so powerful in themselves that they require the simplest narration when it is time to take the reader to the climax. In one of Brecht's last poems, 'And I always thought', there are the lines

> When I say what things are like
> Everyone's heart must be torn to shreds.

When we have made contact with the pervading, dominant feeling in a story or poem and *keep* contact with it, then Brecht is right: the simplest words are enough to tear the reader's heart to shreds.

Now try and achieve this yourself. You have witnessed some appalling incident. Those involved are either too distressed, too wounded or too ill-equipped to say what happened and yet it is vital, for the safety of others, that it be brought to public notice. Describe fully what took place, in a way which will arouse the feelings and sympathy of your readers.

Keeping the connections alive

In Blake's poem and Hemingway's reportage, there is a correspondence between the writer's anger and the conditions that evoke it. The anger is an appropriate response to what the writer describes, a public statement about conditions of life or death. They each address themselves to the reader's understanding of what a just society should be like: they are publicly political writings.

But how do we sustain, in prose or verse, a feeling that is intensely personal, not obviously called up by something 'on the outside' but which seems to be embedded deep within us? Like jealousy, for example?

I think for every feeling, no matter how inward and personal it appears, the writer has to find something in the visible world which corresponds to it, to make it visible for the reader. A feeling has no colour, no outline, no substance of its own. The writer has to give it these things to make it real for the reader.

The things in the 'outside world' which we use to embody or give a shape to our feelings are our metaphors. A dull, cold, rainy day does not literally mean 'sadness' – it is possible to be happy on such a day – but it is so obviously a metaphor for sadness that when it appears in writing it has become a cliché, intended to trigger a predictable response. What we see, or what a character in a story sees, is determined by the frame of mind in which it is seen. When we think of narrative or verse in this way, the underlying feeling assumes a primary importance. So how would we find an outside correspondence for jealousy, a way of writing about it that would make it real for the reader, so real that it puts him/her in touch with his/her own jealousy? To explore this problem, I'm going to talk about two short novels that have jealousy as their central, dominant feeling but are in all other respects wholly different from one another. The first is *Ten-Thirty on a Summer Night* by the French novelist Marguerite Duras, published in 1962.

This novel is about Maria, Pierre and Judith, their child, who are on holiday in Spain with Claire, their young friend. There have been several bad storms on the road and they have decided to break their journey to Madrid and stay overnight in a small town. Maria, a very heavy drinker, has begun to notice signs of passion between Claire and her husband:

> Pierre's hands moved towards hers and then pulled back. Earlier he had made the same gesture, in the car when she was afraid of the storm, the sky rolling over on itself, hanging over the wheatfields.

Although the whole story is written from Maria's viewpoint, no mention is ever made of her jealousy. Pierre's hands are there and what they want to do, and the storm, but not Maria's jealousy. It is enough that we see these things and sit with her while she drinks manzanilla or brandy to wash the sight away (although we are never told why she drinks) – these things are enough to make us participate in what we surmise she must be feeling.

When they all arrive at the small town, police patrols swirl around. The place is electric with drama, with something weighty, weighted down more by the pressure of the storm. A man called Rodrigo Paestra has discovered his nineteen-year-old wife with a lover and shot them both. They are lying in a makeshift morgue, wrapped in brown blankets, and he is still at large. Maria learns from the men she drinks with in the café that he is hiding on the rooftops. So – the magnitude of Maria's feelings is given to us because Duras has come up with another jealous person, whose jealousy was great enough to provoke him to murder.

That night, Maria cannot sleep in the hotel. She is preoccupied with the chimney opposite her balcony, against which a shape is leaning. It looks like a man wrapped in a shroud. It is Rodrigo Paestra. She calls to him, again and again. He doesn't answer:

> She wasn't calling any more. He knew it. Again she opened the corridor door. She saw, she could see them, the others, sleeping cruelly separated. She looked at them for a long time. It hadn't been fulfilled yet, this love. What patience, what patience. She didn't leave the balcony. Rodrigo Paestra knew that she was there. He was still breathing, he existed in this dying night. He was there, in the same place, geographically related to her.
>
> As often happens in summer, a climatic miracle occurred. The fog had disappeared from the horizon and then little by little from the whole sky. The storm dissolved. It no longer existed. Stars, yes stars, in the pre-dawn sky. Such a long time. The stars could make you cry.
>
> Maria wasn't calling any more. She wasn't shouting insults any longer. She hadn't called him ever since she had insulted him. But she stayed on this balcony, her eyes on him, on this shape which fear had reduced to animal idiocy. Her own shape as well.

Her own shape as well. By this tiny brushstroke and by the sky which has suddenly cleared, Duras draws the line of connection between Maria and Rodrigo Paestra. Maria confronts and explores her own jealousy through her obsession with the fugitive on the rooftops. She rescues him, drives him out of town as dawn starts to break and leaves him in a wheat field. She promises to come for him at noon. When she returns to Pierre and Claire, they are unwilling to believe what she claims has happened but they drive with her back to the field and Maria finds the opening in the wheat where he is lying. She is overcome with tenderness towards him, believing him to be asleep. But he is dead. The revolver lies beside him. Pierre comes over and sees him also. Maria and Pierre are the only ones who see him.

Rodrigo Paestra gives a body to the jealousy that lies between Maria and Pierre. In looking at him, Maria sees an aspect of herself, Pierre sees the outcome of the jealousy – a death – and the reader witnesses an internal struggle that has found a public stage. Rodrigo, the storm, the clear night sky, the overwhelming heat in the wheat field, offer Maria's jealousy dramatic correspondences in the world outside. We read her state of mind from the people, the action and the weather of the story.

That's one way of doing it. Another, far more ambiguous and strange way, can be found in Alain Robbe-Grillet's *Jealousy*. Its title in French, *La Jalousie*, means both jealousy and window shutter or blind; so from the outset the reader is taken into a maze of contending meanings. Is the novel about jealousy or about objects? We never really know. We have a narrator who presents us with a plan of his house, obsessively describes the objects therein and the way his wife, always referred to as A. ..., moves about the rooms and onto the veranda. Also present, sometimes, is Franck, a neighbouring farmer, who comes at cocktail hour to drink with A. ... and the narrator. Are Franck and A ... having an affair under the narrator's nose? To a readership schooled in *ménages à trois* from *Anna Karenina* to *Dynasty* it would seem so and yet we are never really sure. We know no more than the narrator, within whose obsessively observant mind we wander, searching, like him, for some sure knowledge. Objects assume an immense importance. They change size. Nothing can be taken for granted. The narrator, like Maria in Duras' novel, reveals nothing directly about the feeling of jealousy. The feeling is represented through his perception of objects, through the way he sees the outside world. So, the jealousy does not form a subject of his thought, one among many, but a lens which filters, colours, interprets everything in its own way:

> It was A. ... who arranged the chairs this evening, when she had them brought out on the veranda. The one she invited Franck to sit in and her own are side by side against the wall of the house – backs against this wall, of course – beneath the office window. So that Franck's chair is on her left, and on her right – but further forward – the little table where the bottles are. The two other chairs are placed on the other side of this table, still farther to the right, so that they do not block the view of the first two through the balustrade of the veranda. For the same reason these last two chairs are not turned to face the rest of the group: they have been set at an angle, obliquely oriented towards the open-work balustrade and the hillside opposite. This arrangement obliges anyone sitting there to turn his head around sharply towards the left if he wants to see A. ... – especially anyone in the fourth chair, which is the farthest away.
>
> The third, which is a folding chair made of canvas stretched on a metal frame, occupies a distinctly retired position between the fourth chair and the table. But it is this chair, less comfortable, which has remained empty.

Although the tone of the narrative seems neutral, empty of feeling, the minute observation of the way A. ... positions the chairs gradually fills it up, so that it begins to pulsate with energy from a subject that is never once mentioned. It is the correspondences that summon forth the jealousy and hold it, throughout the novel, under the reader's gaze, as we witness the perceptions of a mind pulled awry by the pressure of an overwhelming suspicion. Jealousy is called the green-eyed monster: it affects what is seen.

I'm inclined to think that every dominant feeling in a story or a poem affects what is seen and needs to find its correspondences in events and objects outside, which in their turn make the feeling real to the reader. Every feeling has to find the metaphor(s) which will give it a body.

Now is your opportunity to test out the ideas I have put forward in this chapter. First choose a state of mind, a feeling that you know particularly well. Think yourself into it and *hold* it for a while. How does this feeling affect you? How do you see things when you feel this way? In what ways is this different from your other states of mind and being? What could happen when you are feeling this way? What could *possibly* happen?

1. A story is emerging. Write it.
2. A poem is coming into focus. Write it.

8   Myth and Making a Narrative

Where do stories come from? How can you make contact with the force that drives stories, so that your own will contain the mystery and inevitability that causes readers to carry on, fascinated and intrigued during the action of the story, and then satisfied, at the end, that the outcome had to be the outcome, even though they couldn't predict it earlier? Mystery and inevitability: how do you hold these two horses together?

Myths are our first stories. They came down to us before written language was invented, and they are so much to do with the gods, heaven, the earth and her creatures that some people believe that they were given to us by the gods themselves (who sometimes assume the form of animals), and that these gods still move among us, vitalising our lives, explaining to us our tragedies and healing our despair with the power of story.

Such is the argument made by the anthropologist Jeremy Narby, who, in his book *The Cosmic Serpent*, argues that the South American people who eat the tobacco plant and the ahuascara plant, which they think of as the mother of tobacco, see 'the mother of the mother of tobacco' in their visions, and that this mother is a huge snake who guides them in the healing arts and the use of medicinal plants. The cosmic serpent instructs them in their healing.

The structure of myths

If we think of the stories as leading us out of ourselves, as providing altered states of being, as hallucinogenic drugs do, so that we can begin to experience other realities which lie beyond our ordinary sense impressions, then we can see how they can offer us the mystery that will carry our readers on, deeper and deeper into the heart of the problem with which the myth is wrestling. And if we look at the basic structure of myths, we can see how it is always, in essence, the same. Some myths may lack one possible component, but they are all, fundamentally, the same. This is what gives them their sense of inevitability: that no matter how far the hero or heroine has strayed from his or her moorings, there is always a return.

If you examine any novel, play or film, you'll find that it follows the structure of myth. A modernist text may subvert or rearrange the order of mythic moments (Jean Luc Godard said that a film has a beginning, a middle and an end, but not necessarily in that order) and a science fiction novel may rework the question of the hero's return (he or she may be unable to return to a destroyed planet, and so have to discover a home elsewhere), but you will still find the mythic structure informing and driving the action.

According to Aristotle, the basic structure goes like this:

1. Opening
2. Development
3. Climax
4. Turning point
5. Denouement, or untying of the knots.

I will explain each of these in turn.

Opening

The opening, the thing that makes the story possible, consists of some snag or hole in the fabric of everyday life that makes its continuance in its present form impossible. In the story of Oedipus, it is the prophecy that Oedipus will kill his father and marry his mother. That's what makes Laius and Jocasta, his parents, pin his ankles together and put him out on the mountainside to die. In William Trevor's novel, *The Story of Lucy Gault*, it is the attack on the Anglo-Irish house by a group of young republicans. In Ian McKewan's novel, *Atonement*, it is Briony's misunderstanding that her sister is being attacked and raped, rather than engaging in consensual sex. After these acts, nothing can ever be the same again. They form a hole, an opening, through which the story has to happen. The inevitability is already there, in the opening.

Development

In the development, the characters unfold in the different ways they have to because of what the opening has done to them. Oedipus is not brought up as a prince by his own parents, the king and queen, but discovered by a shepherd and given to the king of a neighbouring realm. He develops as a character who doesn't know who his real parents are. We have here the mystery of his birth and the inevitability of his longing to find his birth parents: the two horses, mystery and inevitability, are pulling the story here, too.

In *The Story of Lucy Gault*, Lucy's parents leave Ireland, mistakenly believing her dead, and she is cared for by faithful servants. Her body (like Oedipus, one of her ankles is damaged) and her mind develop in a different way from how they would have if she had been brought up by her own parents.

In *Atonement*, likewise, the characters' lives are changed completely by Briony's childlike misunderstanding. The apparent wrongdoer is sent to prison, and only gets out because he volunteers to fight in France at the start of the Second World War. The older sister, whom Briony thought was being raped, cuts herself off from her family and goes to London to become a nurse.

In all three stories, the family is broken apart by the effects of the opening. We could say that the characters can only develop into unique individuals (as opposed to typical members of a clan or family) because of the strain under which they are placed by the effects of the opening. We could also, therefore, describe the development as a form of initiation, where the main character becomes who she or he uniquely is by enduring a trial or a series of trials.

Climax

The climax can be seen as a false ending. It would be a possible ending if the characters did not have to explore all the implications of the original act and the person they have become because of it.

In Oedipus, we could say that the climax occurs when he, having killed his own father, rids the kingdom of Thebes of the plague by answering the riddle of the sphinx (What goes on four legs in the morning, two legs at noon and three legs in the evening? A man.) and returns unknowingly to the palace of his birth to claim the prize of Jocasta's hand in marriage. He lives with his mother for several years and she bears him children. This is the climax of the myth, the ending that is not an ending.

In *Atonement*, we could say that the climax occurs when Briony herself goes to London to become a nurse, and begins writing the story that will become her own form of atonement for her original mistake. And in *Lucy Gault*, it could occur either when Lucy has the chance of marriage and refuses it, because her own atonement is to wait for her parents to return – the parents she sees herself as responsible for losing – or perhaps it occurs when her father returns, her mother having died in Europe. Here, the climax and the turning point merge together.

Turning point

The turning point is the beginning of full knowledge for the main character, when he/she ceases to see the world in the way he/she has heretofore, without the illusions or limitations of vision that have vexed or eased his/her life. It can involve the near-death of the main character as he/she struggles to take in what he/she has learnt.

In Oedipus, the turning point comes when he learns who he is: his wife's own son, and that he has indeed killed his father. Jocasta hangs herself and Oedipus puts out his own eyes in response to being forced to see so clearly.

In *Atonement*, Briony is compelled to see things as they really are when she attends the wedding of the real rapist with the young woman he raped. Or perhaps there was no rape here either, and the girl just pretended she'd been sexually attacked because she was only fifteen when it happened. Briony realises now just how far her own understanding was from what actually took place, and continues the process of research and discovery that will take her through to the end of her writing life – because she has become a writer in response to the consequences of her original mistake, and writing is posed as a possible reparation for the pain of guilt.

Lucy, in William Trevor's novel, experiences her turning point when she realises, after her father's return, that the course of events was not really her own fault (how can a young child be responsible for the accidental loss of her parents?) and that she has wasted many years in a fruitless waiting to make reparation. Because there is no wrongdoer, only a series of wronged people, including most particularly Lucy herself.

Denouement

I have always greatly enjoyed denouements. When I was a child I used to watch an American series called *Bonanza*, where a man lived with his three sons on a farm called The Ponderosa. They got into all kinds of trouble with cattle rustlers, the army and people who in those days we called Red Indians. At the end of every drama they would all sit around the kitchen table at The Ponderosa and explain to one another how it had all taken place, and how they'd managed to get out alive yet again, which they always did. It was a moment of calm euphoria as they poured themselves coffee and commented on the action, as if they were their own Greek chorus, passing balanced judgement (well, as balanced as it could be in those days, which isn't saying much) on the storm they'd just weathered. So I tend to think of the denouement as the Ponderosa Moment, where all questions are answered and any remaining mysteries resolved.

In many Greek tragedies, the chorus itself explains to the audience anything we might still not understand, and in Oedipus we see the blind king give up his kingdom in order to better understand the hand that fate dealt him and his own part in it. Greek plays are wonderful in the way they explore the line between fate and personal responsibility. They ask: Is there anything we can do that has not been pre-ordained? And when there is, then that point becomes the point of growth of the character's identity. Oedipus isn't really Oedipus until he's suffered everything that fate can throw at him. After he's learnt it all and put out his eyes, then he can become himself. The characters in Greek tragedies, and in Shakespeare's tragedies too, tend to become completely who they are when they've lost everything. And it is precisely the process of losing everything that has brought them to themselves. The journey, no matter how far it took them, was really a voyage into the heart of the self.

In *Atonement* and *The Story of Lucy Gault*, both Briony and Lucy are aware of how much they've lost, and respond in similar ways. Both these ways involve a denouement, an untying of the last remaining knots. Briony finds a copy of the play she was trying to direct when she made her original mistake, and the family is brought together again, minus the two who were wronged, whose lives were cut short because of the wrong. Briony is old now and knows that she is ill, with an illness that eats away memory, but nevertheless something has been saved: some memories, some joy.

Lucy, in her own story, goes back to the source of her loss, to the young man her father shot and wounded when he was attacking their house. This young man has himself become haunted by the consequences of his actions, and spends the end of his life in the local mental hospital. Lucy goes to visit him regularly, and follows his coffin when he dies. Both women return to the original wound and do what they can to heal it. They can't turn back time, they are prisoners of their fate in that sense, but they can do what they can to make amends, and this is how they go beyond their fate and become themselves. It is here that their characters transcend their fate.

I have examined only three stories in the light of Aristotle's narrative structure, but now you may want to cast your thoughts over your own favourite novels, plays and films to see if the structure applies. Remember that the narrative events don't always occur in the same order. The turning point might come in the development, or the denouement might be taking place all the way through. We've had the conventional order of things overturned so many times that the overturning no longer surprises us. It's useful, however, to hold the structure in our minds, ready for when we need to use it.

The hero's journey

We can now turn to another narrative shape, one related to Aristotle's but which is at the same time more detailed, and can therefore offer us more complete guidance in the writing of our own myths, our own stories. It is an order put forward by Joseph Campbell in his book *The Hero with a Thousand Faces*. Originally published in the late 1940s, Campbell was concerned that, as the Nazis had used myths in a regressive, brutalising and destructive way (turning heroes into members of the master race, for example), their vibrant, creative force could be under threat, with people turning away suspiciously from stories that could offer them strong sources of energy and understanding.

Campbell's immense scholarship – he spent his whole life studying them – enabled him to look at myths from all over the world and see their common elements. As the title of his book suggests, his belief was that every story contains the same components, and that each one links the hero's or heroine's own drama with the drama unfolding in the world outside. No writer need ever worry, therefore, that her story is too specific or too personal to have any significance beyond herself, because every story reflects and remembers every other. Campbell believed that dreams are private myths, and myths are public dreams. Even in our dreams, it appeared to him, we are connected to the great stories, all of which are connected structurally with one another. Whatever you write, in a sense, will be part of the mythic pattern.

The pattern Campbell put forward falls into three main categories – departure, initiation and return – with several sections under each heading. You can see from the names of the categories that this pattern carries more of a sense of the journey than Aristotle's, and this is perhaps particularly relevant in cultures that involve a lot of movement and mobility. People migrate from country to country, refugees are forced over national boundaries, people rarely stay still. And in America, the country that has become a home for so many of the world's homeless and which almost destroyed its own native inhabitants in the process, the journey has become the dominant way of describing all the films that are its major creative popular form. Joseph Campbell himself was consulted in the making of *Star Wars*, one of Hollywood's blockbuster mythic movies. You can see his hand in it, especially when the young hero Luke Skywalker discovers that his father is the fallen Time Lord, Darth Vader. It is when Luke has to acknowledge the darkness he was born with that things really start to hot up.

The stories Campbell spent his life reading may have been about gods and goddesses, heroes and heroines, but when you write your own myth, remember that these figures are all aspects of your own psyche. In Campbell's *Ten Commandments of Reading Mythology*, he says: 'Read myths in the first person plural: the Gods and Goddesses of ancient mythology still live within you.'

Here is the mythic structure Campbell identified as common to all the world's great stories. Think of the whole as possible aspects of your own, or your character's adventure. However dark the story that unfolds, or however held within the bounds of daily life, adventure is its essence and its source of energy.

The adventure
Departure:
- The call to adventure

- Refusal of the call
- Supernatural aid
- Crossing the threshold
- The belly of the whale

Initiation:
- The road of trials
- Meeting with the goddess
- The woman as temptress
- Atonement with the father
- Apotheosis
- The ultimate boon

Return:
- Refusal of the return
- The magic flight
- Rescue from without
- Crossing the return threshold
- Inhabiting two worlds
- Freedom to live

I have used this mythic structure in intensive writing courses, which I run over a week and where writers write, read out and discuss their work every day, and have discovered it to offer an incredibly powerful series of catalysts for writers. It takes each one to the heart of their deepest concerns, and seems to compel them to work with difficult but potent material. The structure puts you in touch with the main stages in all the world's great stories, as you will see when your mind begins to play with the subtitles.

But in order to be filled with the story, you need, paradoxically, first to allow your mind to become completely empty. It needs to be empty before it can be filled. Because if it's dodging around with all its usual worries and obligations, the story won't come. 'My little fish has gone into hiding', said Virginia Woolf when some jobsworth came to tell her to get off the grass. So find a quiet room, turn the telephone off, and just sit. Breathe deeply, from deep within your body, for five minutes. Plant your feet firmly on the ground so you are balanced and centred, and just allow the air to move freely in and out of your body. If you can't do this at home, go to a library or any public space where people will leave you alone. As you breathe, wrap yourself in your own privacy.

Departure

Now focus on the first stage of the adventure, which is departure. Your character is living his or her ordinary life, and from somewhere comes the *call to adventure*. Where does it come from? In the ancient myth of the seasons that we know as Demeter and Persephone, the call just emerges out of nowhere, with the lord of the underworld appearing in his chariot out of a fissure in the earth, and carrying Persephone away with him before she has a chance to *refuse the call* or *ask for supernatural aid*. The great myths of abduction all tend to have this quality of suddenness, in which several stages are compacted into one. In this myth, it is Demeter, the mother goddess, who refuses the call and has to spend a great deal of time searching before she can be reunited with her daughter, who is really an aspect of her own self.

Thomas Moore, in his book *Care of the Soul in Everyday Life*, writes:

> I've also known several women who have experienced this myth as a transformation in their lives. They began as naïve, Persephonelike girls, but then fell in with dark men, an underworld of drugs and criminality, and sexual experimentation they never would have considered before. One woman, I recall, had a series of dreams in which a faceless, threatening man was hiding in shadows at the bottom of staircases. She had been quite innocent, but over a period of two years she changed, becoming more complicated and more worldly. Her abduction was from within.

When an actual abduction has occurred, either to the writer or to somebody who is central to their lives, then the desire to use this myth and the accompanying fear of using it may be very great. One year, with no prompting whatever from me, almost the whole writing group worked on the myth of their own abduction. Each one encouraged the others – bravery triggers bravery – and some wonderful stories emerged.

Because the myths address types of behaviour that are often seen as taboo, they can help writers to call up the dark materials that are the source of powerful stories. There is little we can imagine that does not already exist in a mythic story: chopping up and eating your own children, eating yourself, being blinded because you told the truth, dragon's teeth turning into warriors, being walled up alive because you wanted to bury your brother, a bridal gown that burns all the flesh off your body – you name it, it happens in a myth. Myths bravely take us into parts of ourselves that we are both afraid of and fascinated by – they are therefore encouragers of the best stories. So when you yourself, as writer, receive the call to adventure that myth offers, don't refuse it. Look at the way your character tries to refuse it instead.

In *The Epic of Gilgamesh*, the first story ever written down, we have a myth which is the origin of all our buddy movies. It involves the pride of Gilgamesh, king of Uruk, and the journey he has to take before he comes to accept his own mortality. His ordinary life (which involves having the first night with every bride before her husband) comes to an end when his subjects ask the gods for justice and the gods create Enkidu, a wild man whose task is to tame the king and put an end to his abuse of power.

Gilgamesh's own *call to adventure* occurs when Enkidu challenges him to leave the palace and fight with him in the dark streets of Uruk. In this myth it is the subjects themselves who have received *supernatural aid*, and Gilgamesh *crosses his threshold* in order to have his absolute power challenged. Remember what Joseph Campbell said about myths being public dreams. In your dream you are everyone. You are the king who abuses his subjects, and you are the subjects who suffer. You are also the wild man who comes to their aid.

This is true in the Persephone myth too. The innocent girl, the protective mother and the king of the dead who kidnaps the innocent – they are all aspects of humanity that are contained to some degree within everyone. No one is purely innocent, or purely wicked. This was shown to powerful effect in Ariel Dorfman's play *Death and the Maiden*. The doctor who has abused and tortured the woman prisoner becomes *her* prisoner, all the while maintaining his innocence, until the audience is unsure whether she is exacting a just revenge, or is simply mad. When the denouement occurs and the doctor explains why he loved to exert cruel power over the prisoners, we begin to understand this dark part of the psyche. All the great stories seek to shed some light on the dark place. They don't pretend they don't exist.

I think that the key to this first stage in the adventure is the *crossing of the threshold*. The hero or heroine has to leave the confines of home and step out into what he or she doesn't know. If the *call to adventure* is refused, as was the case with Jonah in the Old Testament, they may have to enter the *belly of the whale*, a dark time of constriction and reflection, akin to the time that James Joyce is exploring in

A Portrait of the Artist as a Young Man. If the *call is refused*, or is impossible for some other reason, then the hero is pushed back into himself, to think about the implications and possible consequences of not setting out. The poet Fernando Pessoa's words are relevant here: 'If I had turned left instead of right, if I had said yes instead of no, then the whole universe would be in a slightly different place.' Every act, and every non-act, is significant. Even if your heroine does nothing, that nothing still creates its effects.

It's hard to tell whether Persephone's time in the underworld is her period of incarceration, her *belly of the whale* time. The story is so ancient and so shadowy that it offers itself to our own projections for completion. Perhaps Persephone wanted to leave Demeter, goddess of crops and harvest and perhaps a very bossy mother. Perhaps she had already been trysting for some time with Hades. Perhaps she'd always wanted to be queen of the underworld, and Hades' abduction was her only way of getting away from home. Some scholars believe that Hades himself is a mask for Dionysus, an incredibly old god, equal in power and fertility to Demeter. One can understand his attraction more easily in this case.

Initiation

Whatever the case, whether she jumped or was pushed, it does seem that Persephone's time in the underworld constitutes her second stage, her initiation. In Aristotle's terms, we would call this the climax, because it is where most of the action takes place.

Initiations, in Western cultures, are terrifying times. In traditional cultures they are managed by the elders, and whatever violence occurs is kept within limits by them. The adolescent boys may be made to drink alcohol and dance all night with the older men, their faces scarified to signify their ascent into manhood. The young girl may be made to sit in a small hut for three days, alone, to indicate that her drama will take place inside her own body.

But all this is turned upside down in so-called modern cultures. The elders don't officiate or control the events, and the young ones are left to get on with it on their own, often with dire consequences. One young man's initiation may involve the deaths of all his close friends in a drunken joyride, and a young girl's may be getting drunk at a rock concert and becoming pregnant by someone whose name she can't remember, or never knew.

We could say that this is close to what happens in the myths of Gilgamesh and Persephone. Gilgamesh fights in the streets with Enkidu, they are evenly matched in strength, but Enkidu gives in to the king and they become friends. This sets the scene for a mixture between a buddy movie and a chain-saw massacre. The boys have nothing to hold them back, so they commit sacrilege by cutting down the sacred cedar of Lebanon, killing the Bull of Heaven and terminally annoying Ishtar, goddess of sex and aggression, when Gilgamesh refuses her advances. Their initiation involves everything except atonement with the father, which we could say is imposed from above when the gods decide that enough is enough and one of the dynamic duo must die. You can see that the lineage of this myth leads directly to the violence Quentin Tarantino explores in his films. The lack of an ordering principle (which is present even in *The Godfather*) means that the hero must finally face death without the comfort of any controlling intermediary.

Persephone, on the other hand, experiences her initiation within her own body. She is pregnant by the god and so eats six pomegranate seeds. It is the number of seeds that will determine how long she remains underground, as queen of the dead, and how long she can stay on earth, a maiden again, as Demeter's daughter. In a sense, she herself embodies all the stages in her own initiation: the *goddess she meets* with is herself, whom she must recognise as queen. She herself is *the temptress* who causes Hades to leave his dark realm to find her. The *atonement with the father* is the atonement with Hades, the father of her own child, and Persephone's *apotheosis* is her transformation from dutiful daughter to the glorious and terrible queen of the dead. The *ultimate boon* she receives is her freedom to come and go between the living and the dead, the freedom all women possess as they move between the states of maiden, mother and crone, although they only possess this freedom once they become conscious of it.

Gilgamesh's *ultimate boon*, if it can be called that, is the gift to break the heart: his friend Enkidu's death. After this, Gilgamesh wanders for years. He meets Shiduri, a wise goddess who tells him about Ur-shanabi, the boatman who can cross the waters of death. Once the boatman has taken him over, Gilgamesh talks with Uta-naphisti, the Sumerian Noah, who has been granted immortality. Gilgamesh himself longs to transcend the mortal coil (we could say that all his big bad deeds are an attempt to win immortality) but he learns that the gods have rejected his wish – surprise, surprise. And although Uta-naphisti gives him the Herb of Rejuvenation, this is stolen by a serpent when Gilgamesh gets back to earth. At the end of the epic, Gilgamesh goes back to Uruk and gets ready to die.

It's a strange story, isn't it? Whereas Persephone accepts all the stages in her own initiation, Gilgamesh, a headstrong, awkward customer, rejects all his, particularly any initiation by the female, and has to continue his road of trials into the underworld. And although he has his *magic flight* (with Urshanabi, the boatman) and his – partial – *rescue from without* (the gift of Uta-naphisti), and he *crosses the return threshold* and gets back to Uruk, he hasn't learned to *inhabit two worlds*, as Persephone has, and he hasn't gained the *freedom to live* that comes from experiencing trials and enduring them. All he's learnt, it seems, is that he will have to die, like any normal human being.

You can see from these two ancient myths that the categories within each stage of the adventure can occur in any order, and that your own hero or heroine can refuse to undergo any stage, although a refusal may well disrupt the integrating power of the story. If there is no atonement with the father, for example, or if the hero or heroine cannot become a mother and a father to themselves, it may be impossible to achieve the freedom to live which is the final goal of the journey.

Return

At the end, all the stages and all the figures encountered along the way need to be taken in by the hero if he is to find his final freedom. But this taking-in, this integration, involves empathy, identifying with each figure in the adventure. If there is no empathy, then the adventure will fail in some degree.

It is fascinating to me that *The Epic of Gilgamesh*, which is 4500 years old and the first story ever written down, involves just such a failure. Useful, too, for a writer to reflect on this, because the failure emerges from one thing: refusal. Gilgamesh's refusal of his subjects' needs; his refusal of all Enkidu could have taught him (Enkidu has learnt about sex and civilisation from Shamhat, a sacred prostitute); refusal of Ishtar, the goddess herself. Above all, is Gilgamesh's refusal to make an atonement with the father – symbolised by the gods who want him to stop overreaching himself. It is fascinating, too, that ancient Uruk is roughly equivalent to modern Iraq, where the refusal seems to go on endlessly, involving forces from all over the world. We continue to participate in the ancient conflicts, whether we are aware of it or not.

The important thing to remember, when considering your own myth, is that if the adventure is to succeed completely, then your hero or heroine needs to bring back, over the return threshold, everything they have gained from their initiation and their return. If they are to be able to inhabit two worlds and gain the full freedom to live (which wasn't available to them before they embarked on their journey), then they have to return as a larger, fuller person than they were when they started out.

This goes without saying. But what will give them this freedom? Only you can know this, because it is your story, and even you won't know yet, because you haven't begun to write it yet. What do you want your heroine or hero to come back with? Empty your mind and consider this. Breathe deeply again over five minutes and allow the story to begin to come to you. Remember that it only needs to come a little at a time. You don't need to know the whole thing. Indeed, it may be better if you don't, because then you too, like your reader, can be open to the wonder of the story as it unfolds. When I myself was suffering from loss of faith in a story, Leah, a young writer, said to me: 'You only have to sit at your desk and wait. It will begin to unroll. They always do. You just have to sit and wait.'

So just sit down at your desk. It doesn't matter if you don't have a thought in your head. Soon an image or a phrase will come to you. Write it down. Then wait for the next one. And if nothing is coming at the moment, keep going to your desk every day until it does. It soon will.

9 Developing your Narrative

We now come to the question of the long narrative, the novel, and how we can approach the writing of one. I must admit that this is the fence I do not want to jump, for although I know there are new novels that succeed, I am at something of a loss to describe, in reasonable critical terms, *why* they succeed. The novels that have moved me most (Tillie Olsen's *Yonnondio*, F. M. Mayor's *The Rector's Daughter*, Alice Walker's *The Color Purple*) leave me with the impression that a miracle has happened – a 'How could it be done? Oh! She has done it.' I am surprised whenever a good novel comes to be written because I understand the odds against which it was written.

If we think of the great nineteenth-century novels, published at a time when the novel as a form was still new, but confident, secure in its legitimacy as a writing form, we know that *that* kind of novel could not be written today. In narratives as diverse as *Jane Eyre* and *Great Expectations*, we are aware, when reading, of a certain inevitability of outcome: the writer has us by the hand – *in* his or her hand, almost – and we know we will be led, not necessarily to a happy conclusion but that the narrative will be resolved at a place that feels safe and right, that leaves us satisfied. We know we have been reading a novel but nevertheless we can believe that what the author has told us is true. Perhaps not the literal truth (it is unlikely that Jane Eyre, the unloved orphan, should come into a fortune and gain mastery over Rochester who was once her master or that Pip should be 'raised from his station' by a mysterious benefactor, who turns out to be Magwitch, the convict he once fed), but what Henry James called 'the truth of the imagination'.

Dickens' genius lies in his ability to show, in his novels, the social connections which would otherwise have remained buried. In the lawyer Jaggers' office, Pip sees the death mask of Estella's mother, a murderess. He has to recognise that this young woman, his object of adoration, was born to a mother who had been driven to murder. He has to recognise that his own mysteriously found wealth comes from Magwitch, who, after his transportation, made a small fortune in Australia. The respectable rich are compelled to look at the origins of their wealth, and at their own origins, which lie in crime, exploitation – in the unseen, unmentioned parts of Victorian society. Dickens manages to see life steadily and see it whole.

How can that be done now? Remember that Dickens was writing before Freud had begun to uncover the immense complexity of the human personality, before William James's pioneering work on consciousness, which showed that our conscious mind is not solid but that it runs like a stream, swirling endlessly around symbols, associations from the past; always moving, never at rest. Dickens was writing before Marcel Proust and James Joyce, in their different ways, represented this endless swirling in fiction. Before the First World War, which slaughtered a whole generation of men. Before the Great Depression, which shook so fundamentally any belief in the possibility of continuous economic growth. Before Auschwitz, which shattered any previous, optimistic belief about human nature. After all this, how can the novelist still see life steadily, still see it whole?

For Virginia Woolf, it was the First World War that *broke* something undefinable, something precious, in social intercourse:

> Before the war at a luncheon party like this people would have said precisely the same things but they would have sounded different, because in those days they were accompanied by a sort of humming noise, not articulate, but musical, exciting, which changed the value of the words themselves ...
>
> Shall we lay the blame on the war? When the guns fired in August 1914, did the faces of men and women show so plain in each other's eyes that romance was killed? Certainly it was a shock (to women in particular with their illusions about education, and so on) to see the faces of our rulers in the light of the shell-fire. So ugly they looked – German, English, French – so stupid. But lay the blame where one will, on whom one will, the illusion which inspired Tennyson and Christina Rossetti to sing so passionately about the coming of their loves is far rarer now than then. One has only to read, to look, to listen, to remember.
>
> *A Room of One's Own*

A writer must face the terrifying complexity of contemporary life if his or her fictions or poems are to be relevant to the world today. That means keeping one's ears and eyes open, it means not looking away but acting as a *witness*. But how, you may say, does one begin?

Proceed from the bits and pieces

Yeats writes:

> I must lie down where all the ladders start:
> In the foul rag-and-bone shop of the heart.

The poet H. D. (Hilda Dolittle) writes:

> I go to where I am loved
> into the snow
> with no thought
> of love or duty.

Adrienne Rich writes:

> If you can read and understand this poem
> send something back: a burning strand of hair
> a still-warm, still-liquid drop of blood
> a shell
> thickened from being battered year on year
> send something back.

The writer-self tunnels back into the foul rag-and-bone shop of the heart, into the lumber room, dark and sometimes frightening, where memory dwells. Memory is not abstract. It is made of bits and pieces, sometimes called junk. These are your materials, the things you begin with. You take them out to another place, into the snow, where the light is winter-bright and you can see very clearly. In this light the junk undergoes a transfiguration. It shines, it becomes something very precious, a gift you touch, caress and give back to your reader: something worth having. Writing is your imagination's rescue work. Is there anything too vile to bring out into the light? No. When it is aired it looks and feels different. It has a use. Not just for you – because writing is never *merely* therapeutic, although a healing does occur – but for your readers too.

So, at the start of Tillie Olsen's *Yonnondio*:

> The whistles always woke Mazie. They pierced into her sleep like some gutteral-voiced metal beast, tearing at her; breathing a terror. During the day if the whistle blew, she knew it meant death – somebody's poppa or brother, perhaps her own – in that fearsome place below the ground, the mine.
>
> 'God damn that blowhorn,' she heard her father mutter. Creak of him getting out of bed. The door closed, with yellow light from the kerosene lamp making a long crack on the floor. Clatter of dishes. Her mother's tired, grimy voice.

I don't know whether Tillie Olsen lived near a mine in her childhood. Perhaps she did or perhaps the mine is a gathering together of memories – of being shut in, starved of air, light, freedom of mind and body. It has a physical reality at the same time as a metaphorical reality. Perhaps she started from the feeling and then found a correspondence for it in the outside world. At all events, it enables her to explore the *danger* that shoots through many childhoods: the fear of losing a mother or a father, the conflict we often endure as we hear their exasperated voices arguing above our heads or while we are in bed.

Gabriel García Márquez's *A Hundred Years of Solitude* also begins with a childhood but it engages with a quite different feeling:

> Many years later, as he faced the firing squad, Colonel Aureliano Buendía was to remember that distant afternoon when his father took him to discover ice. Macondo was a village of twenty adobe houses, built on the bank of a river of clear water that ran along a bed of polished stones, which were white and enormous, like prehistoric eggs. The world was so recent that many things lacked names, and in order to indicate them it was necessary to point. Every year during the month of March a family of ragged gypsies would set up their tents near the village, and with a great uproar of pipes and kettledrums they would display new inventions. First they brought the magnet. A heavy gypsy with an untamed beard and sparrow hands, who introduced himself as Melquíades, put on a bold public demonstration of what he himself called the eighth wonder of the learned alchemists of Macedonia. He went from house to house dragging two metal ingots and everybody was amazed to see pots, pans, tongs and braziers tumble down from their places and beams creak from the desperation of nails and screws trying to emerge, and even objects that had been lost for a long time

appeared from where they had been searched for most and went dragging along in turbulent confusion behind Melquíades' magical irons.
'Things have a life of their own,' proclaimed the gypsy with a harsh
accent. 'It's simply a matter of waking up their souls.'

Tillie Olsen's novel begins with the whistle breaking into Mazie's
sleep and Márquez's with the firing-squad, ice and magnets. It is as
if each writer had taken the memory of some powerful event (the terrible shock of being woken by a piercing noise; discovering the
'magical' properties of magnets) and daydreamed in such a concentrated way about it that a group of people, a situation, a story began to
emerge. The story may, when it is 'out', bear only a passing resem-
blance to the writer's own life (although Márquez, at least, has admit-
ted that his novel is firmly grounded in memories of his own
childhood) because of the transforming power of the daydream. But it
is the memory that sits like a kernel at the heart of it all.

In *A Hundred Years of Solitude* we even sense that the writer wants
to take us back into childhood, into the time when 'the world was ...
recent'. The world *is* recent at the dawn of human history and also at
the start of a child's life because at both times it is perceived by new
eyes. At both times things lack names and it is necessary to point. At
both times we see the world with a clarity that we later lose. By
conflating childhood with mythic time – and does not the world
possess mythic proportions when we are small? Are not adults figures
of great power, who can help us grow or else destroy us? Are they not
gods, to the child? – the writer enables the reader to go back, to see
again what we once saw, but this time with the eyes of an adult, the
adult who *regards* the child in him/herself.

Daydreams and their purposes

In *The Interpretation of Dreams*, Sigmund Freud had this to say about
daydreams:

> Like dreams, they are wish-fulfilments; like dreams, they are based to a
> great extent on impressions of infantile experiences; like dreams, they
> benefit by a certain degree of *relaxation of censorship*. If we examine
> their structure, we shall perceive the way in which the wishful purpose
> that is at work has *mixed up the material* of which they are built, has
> rearranged it and formed it into *a new whole*. They stand in much the

same relation to the childhood memories from which they are derived as do some of the *Baroque palaces* of Rome to the ancient ruins whose pavements and columns have provided the material for more recent structures.

(my italics)

I cannot emphasise enough the importance of daydreams for the writer in you. They occupy the time that *seems* vacant, as if you were just hanging around doing nothing – but where in reality the well is filling up, where you are gathering together the material that will make up your narrative; rearranging it, transforming it. What Freud called the *wishful purpose* could also be called the *structuring principle*. It is able to build a palace out of a ruin; it is the shaping spirit of your narrative.

In this chapter we've been looking at two novels which, although they both contain their own particular stylistic innovations, nevertheless stick to the recognised, traditional shape of the novel. They look like any other novel if you just flick over the pages and they are divided into chapters. But what if *your* wishful purpose is not taking you in this direction? Well, fortunately, new ground has been broken by some of our novelists, ground which can be husbanded by new writers. Publishers now accept novels which are composed of a series of short, interlinked stories, novels where prose narrative alternates with poems and – perhaps most interestingly – the epistolary novel has been resurrected, along with the novel of fragments, where every page contains a separate 'statement' that is linked to every other statement through place, character and feeling. Alice Walker's *The Color Purple* is an example of the first and Monique Witting's *The Lesbian Body* of the second.

You are standing on the edge now. You know what can be done in a novel. You have examined the work of other authors, which I called to your attention only to indicate the avenues that are open to us, not to say. 'This is great writing: emulate it.' I don't know what great writing is. I only know what moves me. You now know, to some degree, what moves you and gives you pleasure. You have found things from your past that you can use. You know the power of the daydream to transform the lumber room's contents into precious jewels. Lie down. Roll your eyes back to slow your mind down.

Open the door of the lumber room. The air is thick with dust, accumulated over years of not-remembering, years of not wanting to

know. You can hardly breathe at first. You are afraid and full of excitement at thoughts of what you might find. You feel around in the dark.
There is only a tiny crack of light under the door. Not enough to see
by. You stumble. Your foot has encountered something hard/some-
thing soft/something wet/something dry. You reach down, feel it, lift
it up gently. You do not know what it is. All you know is that you want
it. It is the fragment that will lie at the heart of your novel. You carry it
out into the white, shimmering light. You look at it, wonderingly.

What is it? What, or whom, does it call to mind? Whom does it
summon forth? They are coming, all of them. There is a company of
characters drawn to the object. Who are they? What is their connection to one another? They are talking. What do they say? The object
somehow binds them all together. It possesses a history, a knowledge.
What is this knowledge? Their eyes are wide open as they pass the
object round. It means something different to each of them and they
are all astonished. Why? What is the drama? When did it happen?
What started it, or who?

You are utterly prepared for this and utterly ignorant. The writing
work you've done as you followed the course of this book has laid the
foundations for the palace you're about to build. You opened the door
of memory early on, engaged with your early fears, your early tri-
umphs. You learned the potency of place, the joy of movement, the
way each sense participates in the pleasure of writing. You taught
your people to speak, you learned about the shape of stories. You
learned to keep the feeling high, to communicate with the energy of
your reader. All this will help you.

But there is a sense in which it won't. This, this novel, this *place* you
are going to inhabit, is unknown, uncharted, to anyone except you. *And
you have forgotten the way.* You are sure you knew it once but now it is
so hazy. Will you lose yourself? What will you discover? You need a map.

Make a map. Draw the shape of your novel. Name your people and
make clear to yourself how they are connected. Draw in the events,
make a chart of how they build to the climax. Name to yourself the
climax, so you know what you are writing towards. The map may
prove to be inadequate. You may find a stream, a cave, a factory, a
prison you did not know was there but which insists upon itself as
a landmark. No matter. You need a map to start with, if only for
security, like a childhood blanket or toy weapon. Make a map. Now
discover the name of the country. Where is this novel happening?

Now you are beginning your novel.

10   Writing Poetry

Poetry is the writing form that is nearest to music, and nearest to dance. Lyric poems were originally sung to the lyre by Sappho and her young women on Lesbos, and it was on the shores of Lesbos that the lyre of Orpheus was washed up after Orpheus himself had been ripped to pieces by the Bacchae, the wild women who followed Dionysus, god of wine.

Orpheus used his lyre to try to bring Eurydice back from the underworld after she had been killed by a snakebite. Singing with his lyre, he charmed the lords of the dead. They realised that it is better to be a slave, even, and be alive, than to have lordship over all the hosts of the dead, because a slave on earth can hear music, can take joy from singing, whereas it is quiet in the land of the dead.

Orpheus lost Eurydice. Hades, god of the dead, allowed him to lead her back to the earth, but he had to promise not to look round to check that she was still following him. He heard so many fearsome moans and cries that in the end, disregarding the advice of Hermes, god of thieves and tricksters, who had come with him, he did turn, only to see her pulled back down into the underworld. He followed her back and tried to persuade Hades to give him another chance, but he had left his lyre behind, near the opening to the earth, so he had no means of persuading the lords of the dead, and his pleas went unregarded.

When Orpheus returned to our world he refused to sing or play his lyre. The followers of Dionysus were furious that he denied them the wonder of his music and tore him apart, as was the custom among the Bacchae, whether or not they got their own way. It was the lyre of the dismembered Orpheus, according to Greek myth, that appeared in Lesbos, and so began the great story of lyric poetry.

If we delve into this wonderful myth we can follow the claims that are made for poetry: it can go beyond the gates of death, it can win back a loved one against impossible odds, it can sway the judgements of the gods. And, if it is denied or withheld, it can drive people crazy and lead them to enraged violence. Large claims, perhaps dangerous ones, indicating as they do the state of *ammirata*, ecstatic amazement, which is entered by the poet as she contemplates the object of her love, and shared by her readers or hearers when they participate in her amazement.

Another story is told about the coming of the Muses, the nine divine female beings who inspired all the arts, from the writing of history (the lowest art) to comedy (bawdy comedy lay at the bottom, under the earth, but another form of comedy stood at the very top of the hierarchy, and was seen as particularly close to God). The story goes that there was a time before the Muses existed, when humankind suffered a great deal, because there was no articulated beauty to give us comfort. But with the coming of the Muses, our sufferings were greatly relieved. It is even said that when the Muses were born, some people were so bewitched that they sang day and night, and could not bring themselves to stop even to eat or sleep, but went on singing until they died. But they did not go down into the dark kingdom of Hades, and they died painlessly. The gods took pity on them and turned them into crickets. And this is why, according to the story, crickets are not troubled by hunger or thirst, but live only for their song and go on singing until they die.

Here we learn more about the dangers of falling in love with song. We think of Janis Joplin and Billie Holiday, Dylan Thomas, Sylvia Plath, Jimi Hendrix, Ann Sexton, Bob Marley – who entered so deeply into their ecstasy that they could not come back, and all we have now is their words or their recordings, singing their pain and their beauty into the air, touching and speaking to our own suffering and joy.

Communal ecstasy still takes place at pop concerts, sometimes further induced by drugs, sometimes not. Dionysus, god of wildness and inebriation, moves among the crowds doing his strange but necessary business. The poet Derek Walcott has said that the real poetry is with the pop musicians now, and we have to admit that even sentimental words, when sung to music with a wonderful melody and/or a compelling beat, will move us to heightened states more easily than poetry that is simply read. Another poet, Robert Bly, uses an ancient Greek instrument to accompany his poetry performances, to remind us that at the beginning the words and the music came together, and that we can hear the music behind the words, and running between them.

All this might make you think that poetry is a likely way of getting yourself killed, and that you'd better steer clear of it. But there is another force at work in the art, personified by the god Apollo. It is he who brings light to us, who takes the sun across the sky on its appointed course, and who guards the marriage bed that loving companions fall into at the end of the day. He is the god of order and shape and discipline. He is at his strongest during the day, whereas Dionysus, as we well know, tends to work his magic more at night. Both Apollo and Dionysus guard and inspire poetry. The divine madness is given shape and form by Apollo's structuring hand, and Apollo's rigidity and tendency to meanness is stimulated into pleasure by Dionysus' luscious grapes. There is a poem called 'Apollo Manages His Muses' by an American poet whose name escapes me, which shows the conflict between order and ecstasy. Apollo is a bright and breezy new management type. He's familiar and avuncular with the nine women, all of whom have red hair and green eyes (clearly Celts, clearly trouble). They do not look at him as he plausibly reassures them that he only needs to make a few changes, a few minor adjustments here and there, and one of them, gazing at a stone she is holding in her hand, asks 'What have we to do with reason / Or the sun?'

Nevertheless Apollo *is* there, nudging the poems into shape, whether we like it or not. We long for shape, because shape is sense and beauty, and shapelessness means we cannot communicate, or anyway not in a form that anyone will want to hear. If we are lucky, and a good poem has a lot of luck in it, we can take the help of both these wayward gods, and, when we are *really* lucky, watch delightedly as Dionysus provokes Apollo and Apollo makes Dionysus sit still for a while. So let's proceed, playing with Dionysus and working with Apollo to make songs, or the nearest we can get to songs, to make words move for us and move us into a state of amazement, where we can ask for the impossible:

> Speak to me in
> code, as you would to a gorilla mute with
> grief. As you would speak to animals,
> softly, knowing you can ease them not with
> words but with the meaning of the music
> under words.

Because there is a music under words, emerging out of the silence that lies between them and enables them to make sense, just as tragedy and comedy inhere in each other and darkness is only darkness because there is also light. It is paradoxical, dialectical: amazing.

The poetry playwork I have devised here comes in five stages. With groups of writers I work concentratedly over five days, starting off playing with words and writing a great deal, dancing the poems out with the wild women, and then towards the end writing less, by concentrating more on the forms and what they can do for the music under the words. So on the last day we write only one or two, because here the work is harder: here we are working to harness the wild dancing energy and infuse it with a loose yet graceful discipline.

But you may find you don't have four hours a day for writing. If this is the case, simply spread the exercises out over a longer time, so the playwork I offer for one day you spread over a week, coming and going with the poems between your regular work instead of sitting down for two whole hours, morning and afternoon. This can be wonderfully fruitful anyway: Adrienne Rich 'crucifies' her poems, sticking them up on the wall with pins, adding to, taking from, transforming them as she comes and goes in the room. And there aren't many better poets than Rich.

If, however, you do have five days, and want to use them for poetry (there are worse ways of spending your time) then work, as we do at the City Lit, from 11 to 1 o'clock, have lunch, work from 2 to 4 o'clock. This gets you used to sitting with the poem as you would with a new friend or lover, someone you are determined to make a connection with. If you get bored or frightened, don't run away, just sit tight until something begins to happen. If you are afraid of committing yourself to the work, don't do anything, just sit. Eventually the fear will subside and you'll be able to proceed with what you most deeply desire.

The first day

Begin with a sound you have heard most often throughout your life: your own name. Say it aloud, say it silently inside your head. What does it make you think of? Whose voice do you best like to hear say it? Follow the associations where they lead you. You are walking far into the wood of your name. Whom do you meet there? Who and what clings to your name? Spend ten minutes thinking and dreaming about the sounds and meanings that build your name, remembering all the time that your name is *you* – if it is. If there is a dissociation between you and your name, if you have changed your name and believe an earlier name to be more completely you, then dream around that dis-sociation. That will fecundate your writing also.

Honour this dreaming time. When the white invaders visited an American Indian chief to tell him that his young men should be spending their days at work, he replied: 'But if they worked all the time, what opportunity would they have for dreaming?' It is the most honoured dreams that make the best songs. Dreamless work makes only mass-produced conveyor belt articles, not masterpieces.

Don't bother about form, and don't worry if the poem comes out as a bit of doggerel. Doggerel is fun, and it means we're not afraid to mess about and be stupid. Stupidity means Dionysus is coming in. You are learning to be an idiot: the hardest, and the best, lesson for a poet.

Here are two name dream poems, one of mine and one of a poet who worked with me over the five days. He came because he felt there was too much order in his work, and he wanted to loosen up:

No other name would smell as sweet

My given name, 'The Gift of God'
has brought scant help to this poor sod.
Small ground for surgical dissection
Borne by both in tomorrow's election.
Then 'Ring', that's a corner of a field
Where Saxon fathers learned to yield.
And an English flower? Well, it may be
tho' the song says they bloomed in Picardy.
Perhaps much better said in prose
by yours, sincerely, John Ringrose.

Julia

I know a woman called Julia a
bit. She seems to know me any
way. When I try to say what she is
like, she does something unjulia. She used
to smoke. That was when she didn't like
herself a bit. When she stopped, she began
to burn. That brought the two Julias
closer. Then came tears. It is the tears
will wash the two together, if any
thing can. Tears to make the nice girl
get to like her unpredictable
twin sister.

Now begin. Write a poem so that, when someone reads it, they will never forget your name. When you have written the poem – give yourself up to half an hour – stand up and read it out loud. Read it in different tones of voice: seriously, sadly, like Peter Sellers reading the words of 'A Hard Day's Night', cynically, questioningly, joyfully. All these tones of voice are you. This is your name, your poem, your voice. And then take a break. Go for a walk. Get yourself a drink of something you like.

The next dream poem is called 'Wish list'. The idea comes from the poet Diana Gittins, who calls it 'Shopping list'. I learnt it during one of her Right Writing Workshops, where she helps people to learn to write from the right-hand side of the brain.

What you do is to think of everything you'd like to have: material things, personality characteristics, qualities of mind and thought, differences of time and world and space. This is a wonderfully useful poem to write, because it gives you what the Americans call your *druthers*, your *I'd rathers*, so aspects of yourself become clear to you that perhaps were not clear before, and you can proceed with more knowledge. It's also great to send as a Christmas or birthday card to your friends. It nudges *them* into thinking what they really want, too.

Here are two examples to start you dreaming:

Wish list

First I thought a road, widening
with some Parthenon crowning each successive hill
Then a green garden with uncertain shades
and sunny clearings: household wine
a half full beaker from the far far south.

A rested mind in a healthier body.
A colour control upgrader to give
insurance against pastel shades.

But most of all I need a key
to open lovely minds
locked in narrow wards or corridors,
to learn to meet others without the spasms
of deep immune response,
rejecting advances like transplanted tissues.

To see themselves as others see them

and learn to love the thing they see;
to hold hands in an unbroken circle
with Mexican waves of laughter
at the worst of jokes, in the worst of taste.

John Ringrose

Shopping list

All the perfumes
or no smell at all
just skin
with a little papaya for breakfast
grey seeds scooped out
filled with lime to hit the roof of my mouth

Pumice for my feet
a flannel for the hard lines
a brush with death
a mortal coil for mosquitoes
the umbilical cords of all my babies

a hill
a confluence of four rivers
Tigris, Euphrates, I forget the rest
a vital spark
a glass of wine
thou, if thou'd come
a garden
with angels at the gate.

J. C.

You might also like to explore your difficulties in saying what you want. Some of us have been denied so many things we need to make us complete human beings that we dread even getting to know our needs. We think there's no point, because we'll never get what we want. Remember that writing can emerge from these kinds of paralysis. We are not doing anything in the real world, but in the imaginary world. They touch, of course, and some people would even claim that the real world is imagined into being by the imaginary world, that we dream our lives into plans and action. But for now, concentrate only on the words to say it. Let the fears come forward and announce themselves. Dream the wants, the needs and wishes into a list. Make the list.

A new species of creature

Now let's turn away from ourselves and into the outer world, to try writing a poem from the other side. Some writers think of poems as spinning out of themselves, as a spider exudes silk through its spinnerets; while others think of them as something *out there*, not inside at all, something the poet has to watch and wait for and eventually capture and make his/her own. Ted Hughes is one such poet:

> There are all sorts of ways of capturing animals and birds and fish. I spent most of my time, up to the age of fifteen or so, trying out many of these ways and when my enthusiasm began to wane, as it did gradually, I started to write poems ... at about fifteen my life grew more complicated and my attitude to animals changed. I accused myself of disturbing their lives. I began to look at them, you see, from their own point of view.
>
> And about the same time I began to write poems. Not animal poems. It was years before I wrote what you could call an animal poem and several more years before it occurred to me that my writing poems might be partly a continuation of my earlier pursuit. Now I have no doubt. The special kind of excitement, the slightly mesmerised and quite involuntary concentration with which you make out the stirrings of a new poem in your mind, then the outline, the mass and colour and clean final form of it, the unique living reality of it in the midst of the general lifelessness, all that is too familiar to mistake. This is hunting and the poem is a new species of creature, a new specimen of the life outside your own.
>
> *Winter Pollen*, pp. 10–12

Perhaps the two ways of thinking about writing poems are related. The 'stirrings of a new poem in your mind' may be an internal reality, interior psychic work that will be done through poetry, which is nevertheless perceived as something moving in the outside world: a projection from the inside on to the outside. However, I still believe it is helpful to consider the poem as another creature, one that is separate from ourselves, something new that we need to wait for patiently before we can come to know its shape, texture and character.

All you need to do for this exercise is focus upon an object, perhaps something nearby, something you can hold in your hand. Place it in front of you. Stare at it. Let your eyes roll into the back of your head so you can see it in your inner landscape. Narrow your eyes so the light hits it in peculiar ways. Go where it takes you. It doesn't need to make sense, in the narrow way we understand sense. It will make its own kind of sense, one you will come to understand later. Because poems tell us things we don't yet know; they give us the kind of news the newspapers can't give. Wallace Stevens said: 'You can't get the news from poems, but men die every day for lack of what is found there.' So take in your object and allow the strange news to come.

Here are two that came in the writing group. They might help you get started:

Still

Pure Spring Water trembles in a plastic bottle
on Ruby's table. Still water. The minerals in each drop:
lapis, punctured neophytes, martyrs
from the bottom of the impure well.
All memories of cotton from the street of slaves.
Slippery water, algaed rocks I slid down
above the abandoned sugar plantations
with my Chinese cousin who'd dive so high
I feared for his neck, that's broken now
since after the hurricane, clearing brush by his stretch of riverbank
a dead tree searched him out and fell
on the deep sea fisherman
who knew how to catch white tuna
so the flesh stayed white
by plunging it in icy water
the moment he'd unhooked it from his line.

J. C.

My glasses case

When new it imitated leather, luxury, desire.
A sleek smooth case for sir's occasional spectacles.
Now the internal edges are frayed
tag ends of white cotton: the glitter, the surface
cracked like the moon, white veins beneath dried earth.
But still showing faintly across the edge
impressed in tarnished silver
'Christian Dior – Monsieur.'

Dior, the torturer of women's bodies
fantasiser of feminine form
New Look, wasp waist, corsetted,
pinched, bone wired, sculptured,
'To wear this gown, Madame needs to be naked underneath.'

My glasses case is naked underneath.
The rough white lingerie of its inner coat
thrusts through the surface
more honest than its namesake's gowns on the fashion walkway.

The shape of the glasses that live in my model case
dictate its form
untrammelled by wires, uplift or flounce.

This battered case now looks
like a Dior gown worn for washing up
or deadheading the garden.
But I keep it: I live with it still,
It has changed of course from a thing of fashion –
is, you might say, familiarised by use.

John Ringrose

Once you have written your poem, again, rest. I can't stress this enough. Poems are your confrontation with what you don't yet know. You enter into an unknown region and you learn to tolerate feeling completely lost. This can be frightening, particularly at first. When you don't know where you are, time seems to move in a different way. You can have been at your desk for ten minutes, yet you feel you've been on a long exhausting journey. You have. The adventures, ardours, labours have been invisible to the outer world, but they are nevertheless real, and tiring. So with each expedition to the unknown, give yourself time to recover. Sit still. Let the new knowledge sink in. The unknown is working its transformation inside you: you need to give it time to do its work.

Thinking about it

Just thinking about poems can make more poetry come. You set out on your journey and, when you return, you consider the journey and the effects it had upon you. You can experiment with moving back and forth between here and amazement, moving between the worlds with greater ease. In the writing group we asked 'What does poetry do?' and gave one another time to make poems about our inner adventures. Here are two we came up with:

> So sad.
> Sitting in the room –
> the four walls, defining.
> Sometimes a voice is raised,
> a coffee stirred,
> sometimes ...
> 'now let's consider what it is that happens
> when a vector pierces the ionosphere
> let us peep into the fulcrum between cause and effect.'
>
> Not me, I said,
> And is that sound, that murmur
> some new thought in your mind,
> a cloud skimming the sky
> or the sleepless clattering
> of guns trained upon Sarajevo?

Peter Godfrey

What does it do?

> It brings me to my knees.
> What am I worshipping?
> There are gods on every petrol station forecourt
> blinding the windows of white Range Rovers.
> Little gods speak across the wires
> through my unlucky telephone number
> telling me of wars I can't prevent
> in cities I can't pronounce the names of
> and it's muddy. The diesel has combined
> with every mote of pollen to make a furious
> enthusiasm in my nose. There's nothing I can do
> but wait for a sound along the abandoned railway track
> of the blackthorn growing, that can kill a man
> if his hand gets pierced by it.

J.C.

As you can see, both these poems took us towards a consideration of death, violence, wartime and the everyday. Dionysus was walking through them, requiring that we imagine piercing and ripping, the destruction we're capable of. But another poem emerged, which looked at the way poetry touches everyday things:

Butterfly wings

There is a force that can
turn the sun into an orange
and the earth into a waltzing walnut

a road into a life
a service station into Xanadu
and make McDonalds a golden altar
tiptoe between heaven and earth

that can see our mother's childhood in a kitten at play
and reach in a child's endless queries
'Why? Why? How?'
to the pole's ozone halo and the hydrogen bomb.

It stretches the spirit across the sky
like strudel pastry
and places the homely toad in the hole
with nectar and manna on fields of asphodel.

It is lost in translation
and interpretation
and on this road
you may have just passed it.

John Ringrose

I like these three poems, but I think there's something partial about all of them: the first two are too much under the sway of the dark god, and the third is a little too bright. The trick I think is to wait until both gods come into the same room with you, and then dance. It is the dance with life and death, chaos and order, dark and light that makes poetry part of the life more abundant. And to dance, we need to learn some steps, whether they are the sedate steps of a galliard or the entranced turning steps of a whirling dervish. Even the wildest dance has its rhythm and its shape.

The second day

The dance we began with was the *renga*. Tim May, one of the writer participants, explains how it works:

Many of the people in the west have heard of *haiku*, those miniature Japanese poems of three lines of 5, 7 and 5 syllables. The most famous of them, by the seventeenth-century poet Basho, goes like this:

Japanese	*English translation*
Furuike ya	The ancient pond.
kawazu tobikomu	A frog jumps in
mizu no oto	– the splash of water.

Haiku developed in the seventeenth century from the *hokku*, the opening section of a much older collaborative verse form known as *renga* or linked verse. A *renga* consists of between two and a hundred alternating parts of 5–7–5 syllables (the form of the *hokku* mentioned above) and of 7–7 syllables (the form of the *wakiku*, the accompanying poem following the initial *hokku*). After the first participant in a *renga* session has written the opening 5–7–5 syllable section or *hokku*, the second participant caps it with a second section or *wakiku* of 7–7 syllables which is in some way thematically linked to the first part. The third participant continues the sequence by composing another 5–7–5 section, followed by the fourth participant's 7–7 section, the fifth person's 5–7–5 section, and so on in alternation. In our case, all this took place on sheets of paper passed around the big table.

It's wonderful if you can write *renga* with others, with friends or in a writing group, but you can also call on different parts of your own self to write the braided verse. What we did was select a title from John Giorno's collection *You Got To Burn To Shine*, a deeply moving book about relationships between people, sex, AIDS, and the experience of dying. The title we chose was from a poem about the last days of his close friend, where he writes about sitting with her and participating in what he calls 'profound gossip'. This phrase arrested me because of the way it turns conventional meanings on their head. We have been taught to think of gossip as banal and trivial, but its root is *god sib*, meaning the advice of the godparents: necessary and wise counselling in how to live our lives. It has become degraded because it is associated with women, but as Maria Warner says, we're all women now because so much power has been taken from us, and as we can't believe what the newspapers tell us, gossip is a good way of finding out what's really going on. And 'Profound gossip' is a good title for *renga* writing because it enables you to throw in things you overheard on the bus, a line from a play, bits of children's speech, all things that will thicken the texture of your writing and create the feeling that you're writing in a real language, one that is all there, alive in the present moment. Here's one that emerged:

Profound Gossip

He said to her *she's*
a dangerous woman, as
someone would who has

a blue knitted cover on
his spare toilet rolls. And I

ask *Do you love him*?
his quick revenge, forgotten
misery, babies

breastfed with evil who refuse
to die. *No*, she says, and

laughs, that I'm now, it
appears, evil intention,
not Saint George. Jane, let's

let that boy of lies spill out
hold our tongues and learn to speak

with hope: that we both
married babies culled from lies
who could not fill the

world with green doormats, who will
not bring Saint George, who refuse

to die, and the beans
will spill out over his spare
toilet rolls, his breast-

fed evil intention, that
we learn to hold our tongues, must

just, causing pain,
offspring disease, because here
is a man who can –

Renga is a way of letting our fingers dance. At times we almost forget about the words, we are so intent on getting the number of syllables right. It is this word-forgetting and self-forgetting that makes poetic form so transformational: in becoming slaves to the form we often discover something we didn't know we wanted to say. It is like acting in the service of a god: our ordinary actions become suffused with joy because we're doing them in his or her service, not our own, and not to conform to anyone else. Service frees us: form liberates the most deeply embedded meanings in the poem. This is Apollo and Dionysus in their best partnership.

On that second day, in the afternoon, we moved from collective Japanese verse to a form that is perhaps the most favoured and most feared in Western poetry: the sonnet. We tried the sonnet next because I believe it's wise to face quickly the things we think we're incapable of, and simply try them out. Think of the sonnet as a game, of counting syllables *and* making rhymes, like juggling silk handkerchiefs and plates at the same time. Or miss out the rhymes if you want to. Peter Porter called the unrhyming sonnet 'that toothache form', but it's a perfectly respectable variation nonetheless. Or, do what Gavin Ewart did. He declared he'd solved the problem of rhyme. You simply use the *same* word at the end of a line, instead of a rhyming word. A Ewart sonnet could be really fun.

Anyway, here's a Shakespearean sonnet, by the man himself, so you can see what he's up to and how he goes about it. I've put letters at the end of the lines so you can more easily discern the rhyme scheme.

Sonnet 138

When my love swears that she is made of truth,	A
I do believe her, though I know she lies,	B
That she might think me some untutor'd youth,	A
Unlearned in the world's false subtleties.	B
Thus vainly thinking that she thinks me young,	C
Although she knows my days are past the best,	D
Simply I credit her false-speaking tongue:	C
On both sides thus is simple truth supprest.	D
But wherefore says she not she is unjust?	E
And wherefore say not I that I am old?	F
O, love's best habit is in seeming trust,	E
And age in love loves not to have years told:	F
Therefore I lie with her and she with me,	G
And in our faults by lies we flatter'd be.	G

You can see that every line rhymes with its alternate line, apart from the last two, which rhyme together. The last two are called a *heroic couplet*. Each line has ten syllables, and the metre is iambic, the limping metre of the lame man. This metre is wonderfully appropriate, especially in Shakespeare's later sonnets, because it underscores the sense that he is bound or hobbled to someone his reason rejects: that his passion is pulling him one way, and his reason another.

Traditionally, the sonnet presents us with a problem in the first eight lines – the octet – and brings about a solution in the concluding six lines – the sestet. You can see that this is the case with sonnet 138. In the octet Shakespeare tells us what's going on, admitting and perhaps lamenting the fact that he and his lover are lying through their teeth to each other. Then the sestet seems to be saying 'But this is all right. This is what lovers do. And then there's the sex.'

Don't be daunted by the sonnet. It's just another form to play with, step into, find your way around in. Two of the writers at the week's summer school wrote dream sonnets, grasping on to the form to help them get lost in their dreams. Here they are:

Sonnetease

I've had two dreams about this man. He thinks
he's welcome in my sleep to share my life.
We trolley down the aisles picking links of
sausages, a Sunday roast. I act the

washing powder wife. He's anxious in the
second dream, he can't make love. The walls suck
in, the carpet's full of come, milk curdles
with white plaster dust from the rose above.

He holds me, sinks his head in my shoulder.
'Why does it have to be like this?' he moans,
The milk has risen to the armchair seat.
We oscillate our heads like blinking fans.

'You should see my period,' I replied.
He's a famous poet I can't abide.

Chrissie Gittins

Dream – A Sonnet

My neighbour's grass is green, brilliant with flowers
Filled with Bill Clinton, smiling, tall and blond.

Beside a man-hole cover, black, sunbaked for hours
Clinton and my neighbour shake each other's hand.
My garden's silk, beset by blight and heat
Withers into a skeletal Marie Celeste
While Clinton, split, breast high in fields of wheat
Becomes a brass band and – I forget the rest.
Why should all this remind me of a dove
That lately nested in a garden tree?
Are grass, great power, wild seas, logos of love
Fluttering, flourishing, not bound, not free?
Perhaps my ship's not lost, rigging still taut,
Drifting, but waking safely into port?

John Ringrose

Can you see the wonderful playfulness that the form has provoked in both these writers? It's as if they can let go, wander entirely into their own uniqueness, their own marvellous strangeness, secure in the knowledge that this ancient form is holding them and won't let them fall.

Now you try. Write a dream sonnet. Or don't even try. Just do it. Let it come in its own way.

The third day

By the third day we were very tired, but as third days are traditionally the days for rising again, and we didn't want to fail the feast, we decided to get down to some physical work and try a villanelle. A villanelle means a 'farm work song'. It has its origins, like the sonnet, in twelfth-century Provence in southern France, and it involves a fair amount of repetition, because many types of work are repetitive and require a strong line to help the labourer do the work again and again. It has ten syllables in each line, and the metre is often iambic (di *dum* di *dum* di *dum* di *dum* de *dum*), the lame walk again, but the more you vary it, the more surprising and fascinating it will be. You need to choose two strong lines, capable of being repeated in alternate verses, and linked enough to come together at the end. These two lines should rhyme. Here is one we wrote, so you can see how the repetitions and rhyme scheme work:

Villanelle

Once on the trail, you can't throw off your pack.	A
The journey's a surprise; you're getting near	b
When the way forward ends in turning back.	C

Forests close in, trolls and wolves attack;	a
the cost of living soars, the future's dear.	b
Once on the trail you can't throw off your pack.	A
You wad it with exotic bric-a-brac	a
exports from Birmingham to old Kashmir.	b
They sent them forward but you bring them back.	C
Halfway you sense another lack,	a
peaks fogged in cloud that once had seemed so clear	b
Out on the trail, you can't throw off your pack.	A
And now you've landed on an earlier track;	a
memories of young ambition, callow, sincere.	b
That way forward's found you turning back	C
to old streets, old dreams, dim hopes, amorphous, slack.	a
The further you fare, the more you face the rear.	b
Once on the trail, you can't throw off your pack	A
even if 'forward' ends in turning back.	C

John Ringrose

Can you see how the villanelle lends itself to a different train of thought from the sonnet? The sonnet leads us into a problem and then a resolution, whereas with a villanelle we turn round and round, seeing a situation from many different angles, with lines A and C, the powerful repetends, implacably returning us to our starting place. The motto for a villanelle seems to me to be T. S. Eliot's 'In my end is my beginning'. It is a form that could help us face something inescapable in our lives, something we cannot change but which we want to see as clearly as possible. Dylan Thomas's villanelle 'Do Not Go Gentle into that Good Night' is an example of this, as is Elizabeth Bishop's haunting poem 'One Art', where she examines her talent for losing things, houses, countries, even the person she most loved. Whereas early villanelles (I'm guessing here) may have contained purely phatic repetends like 'With a yo heave ho and a yo heave ho' or 'And the rain it rains on everyone', in contemporary hands, because we follow in the footprints of psychoanalysis, the repetends often refer us to compulsions or obsessions, longings or actions we repeat without fully understanding why we repeat them. There is often an Ancient Mariner atmosphere in a villanelle, where the poet has to keep telling her tale in repeated attempts to ease the pain inside her.

There was a time, when I was undergoing extremely painful changes in my life, when the villanelle offered itself as the only form I found at all appropriate. Here is the poem that came to me:

What can we sell except parts of ourselves?

I did not exactly sell you. I left	A
you there in the woods of your own free will	b
you with your dog, my daughter, running swift	C
around the house, untroubled by the heft	a
of my thought basket stumbling up the hill.	b
I did not exactly sell you. I left	A
before I could know what it was I left,	a
or that my thought basket would soon be full	b
of you with your dog, my daughter, running swift	C
around the little house, the place I left	a
because of some ache I could not name. Still	b
I did not exactly sell you. I left	A
you with your father knowing you'd be safe	a
but not that I could not be sound. Will	b
you with your dog, my daughter, running swift	C
come back to me, unanchored, lost, adrift,	a
if I can make a home to keep us whole?	b
I did not exactly sell you. I left	A
you with your dog, my daughter, running swift.	C

I took the title from a terrifying story by Sonja Besford, the Serbian writer, which examines a place where people are so desperate that they sell parts of their own bodies in order to buy food and clothing. Don't be afraid to take titles, words, or whole phrases, from others. There are traces, ghosts, footprints of other writing in everyone's work, just as we all breathe air and contain cells that were once part of other people's bodies. In the turmoil of changing continents and leaving my younger daughter behind because I couldn't bear to live in a certain place, I found myself hedged around on every side. If I stayed with her I felt I would die, and having left her I seemed to have literally given away a crucial part of myself. The villanelle didn't offer any resolution to this appalling mess, but it enabled me to face it and get it down in words. When she finally returned I wrote a *rubaiyat*, a totally different kind of poem, a hymn of praise. We tried one of those at the end of our week of writing poems.

But before we leave the villanelle, I want to show you one more, to give you more sense of the range of things it can embrace. This one shocked me into an awareness of the piercing sensuality of the river and the land, the fisherman, his line and the fish:

Desire Villanelle

Out of the shadow, something soft and turning
troubles flies twitching the skin of the lake.
You're the fish in black water, burning

in the axle loins of the angler, warming
his expert finger for the cast and take.
Out of the shadow, something soft and turning

calls the hare to break, bracken stamping
her violent March warning. Forsaken,
you're the fish in black water, burning

your face on a mind white with disowning
ideas. A dead finger on parchment aches
in shadow, for something soft and turning

to settle dreams, dreams, then wet morning
raking light on white dew, cool dew, slaked.
You're the fish in black water, burning

dust off a memory that died, yearning
and a deeper dying lives, unspoken,
out of the shadow, something soft and turning.
You're the fish in black water, burning.

Celia de la Hey

Can you feel the power of the metaphor here? The poet, and you the reader, become the fish desiring the angler, who is himself an aspect of the fish. Something in the fish calls to everything else in the morning: to the hare calling the bracken to life with her powerful back legs. But the fish is also the abandoned lover burning her face 'on a mind white with disowning ideas'. The poet becomes the fish, beloved quarry of the angler, the hare, the abandoned one, the dead finger, the wet morning and finally the memory and the 'deeper dying'. And this is the quality of attention you will learn to allow to emerge in your poems: this way of attending so fully to the object under your gaze that you feel you are merging with it. When you feel yourself ceasing to be yourself as you slide softly into what you are looking at, when you begin to feel what it is like to be that thing, that animal, that person, then the miracle of poetry is working inside you, and you will begin to find ways of enabling the same miracle, the merging of subject and object, to take place in your reader. You have to have felt it yourself before you can communicate it to someone else.

The fourth day

On the fourth day we took time to reflect on what had gone before, to look through all the work we'd done and ask ourselves, in the light of these explorations, What do I want to say? I think this is something that comes clearer to us as we write more. We each possess a unique writing voice whose texture becomes richer and more complex the more we use it; and linked with this is our own unique contribution to the sum of human knowledge. This might sound arrogant, but if you think about it, it has to be true. No one has your genetic inheritance but you, and only you have experienced life with this inheritance through the particular environment you were born into. So only you can know what you know, only you can write it with the authority of your own voice, whose authority grows the more experienced it becomes. With this in mind, it is worth considering what you really want to say, what presses inside you in the desire to be communicated.

This 'really want to' can be either a close meditation on an object, a series of speculations and longings about human conflict, or *anything else*. This is your own particular poem statement, so you can let it come as freely as it wants to. Let the lines begin where they want to and end where they want to; let the poem emerge with its own integrity as you relax and allow it to gradually come into being. Remember that this needs to be said, and only you can say it.

Here is one that came in the group:

Perceptions

I

I want to place this apple precisely
this unnamed child of Cupid's mother.

It is two and three eighths inches high
two, three quarters inches wide across.

The centre dip, Venus's navel,
lies to the left, like her great heart,
So the stalk (nine-sixteenths in length, swelling to a
delicate flat top)
inclines at an angle of sixty-two degrees
to the horizon.

Love's fruit is not crooked
but elegantly bent.
Count the stripes of red like blood
pulsing over sponged russet, green, rag-rolled yellow
and a partial shade of textured brown,
rougher to the touch,
that slides round that voluptuous navel, confirming
that this apple is round, solid,
distinct: unique.

But note that by mischance
blind Cupid's arrow has bored
a tiny tunnel of love (two sixteenths across)
for a gourmet libertine maggot
who waits, curled, to add a new sensation
to love's first bite.

So here is this apple, elegantly bent,
fundamentally flawed
like some loves themselves,
and you can either risk the strange raw taste of experience
or replace it as an icon for contemplation
unfit to eat, but a fit
subject for a poem.

II
When Brecht chose crockery for a play
he always selected
plates that had been used, washed and used again
mugs battered in long service
and tables battle (and bottle) scarred.
The everyday, often overlooked,
nuts and bolts of day by day survival,
Material images of his vision

this agnostic, atheistic poet
held to be
sanctified by use.

John Ringrose

Can you feel the way this meditation on an apple leads the poet into his own sense of what can be eaten or used and enjoyed and what needs to be reserved as an object of contemplation? I particularly like the exploration of Brecht's hand properties in part II, the celebrations of objects (and by association, people) who wear the marks of life and robust use.

Now your turn. What is it you've always wanted to say?

When you've written this poem, put it aside and sit back. Let your mind wander around your poem. Which metaphors enter your thinking to light your way further in? Remember that the metaphor, which lies at the heart of our language, stretches itself between one meaning and another: it enables us to say what we didn't know we wanted to say as we allow ourselves to sink deeper and deeper into likeness, exploring the furthest limits of the way thoughts, feelings, things, animals, people and gods are infinitely joined. Here is the poem that came to John Ringrose. Notice the way metaphor tends to give us the unexpected. It brings us up short, and causes us to see what we thought we knew in a new way:

Metaphors for a feeling

When he saw her he saw:
   a deer running in another herd
   a brown and yellow iris in a rose bed
   a seagull in a flight of Concordes
   a unicorn without a virgin
   seaweed in a city square
   a bunch of asparagus on a baker's shelf
himself:
   standing before a non-reflecting window staring
   at a ruby of his mother.
   Feeding lines of dialogue to a photo cut-out.
   Tied and manacled against a tree
   while the circus parade passed
   Calling, calling to the boat whose time is up,
         but who won't come in.

Learning French because the Greek has moved on.
Sailing to Troy to fetch her back,
only to find she spent the war in Egypt.

John Ringrose

It is metaphor that takes your writing further into its own unique self, because only you can make the connections that come unbidden to your mind when you meditate on something that is important to you. Don't be afraid to stretch the connections as far and tight as you need to. You won't lose the reader. The reader likes to work hard. She or he is like a healthy horse. Working hard to get from one point to another makes her feel more alive, makes her feel the power in her own mind and body.

The fifth day

By the last day of your poetry work you will be tired, but also relieved, perhaps even in a state of celebration. This is the time to try a *rubai* (plural *rubaiyat*), a form that comes from the Middle East and is known best through the long exhortation called *The Rubaiyat of Omar Khayam.*

The *rubai* has four lines, again with ten syllables each. It is a *very* rhyming form, with the line endings going AABA, but you can make as many half or slant rhymes as you like, to make it feel like conversational speech. Indeed, it works even better if you can make it feel like everyday speech, and hide the rhymes so the fact of its being a rhyming poem dawns on the reader very slowly. The *rubaiyat* can take place over as many stanzas as you like, so you can also use it as a narrative poem, to tell a story. This will conceal the poetic form even further; you will make your reader think you are 'just' telling her or him a story, when you are actually singing your most harmonious music. She or he will only gradually realise what you are doing, and by then it will be too late, you will have already worked your magic. This is the best kind of pleasure you can give; it looks effortless, and your reader only understands afterwards the arduous care and skill that have gone into the making of it.

Here is my own celebration written when I realised that Miriam would return to live with me:

Rubaiyat for Miriam

I thought you would not return to me, my
daughter, by your look, your eyes so angry
that I had left you there with your father
while I began to live without the lie.

It seemed a cauterized wound. You had held
a candle to your broken part, to seal
me out. You pulled yourself away, and would
not offer me your hand, I thought you'd healed

yourself, or pushed the wound deeper inside
a poisoned itch your clenched young skin could hide
for years – for ever? – until that last night
when I came to your bed and asked if you'd

let me lie with you a little while. You
rolled your eyes to heaven, then muttered 'Oh
all right, just half an hour'. I watched you fall
asleep, your seven year body letting go

into our last hours together. Then I
slipped my arms around you, thinking *only
this one night. I have to print your face, your body
deep into my mind so I can never*

*Lose the sense of what it's like to have you
here with me.* I did not sleep. There was so
little time, Miriam. Then, towards dawn
you turned to me and seemed to melt. I drew

you very close, you wrapped your arms around
my neck. When you opened your eyes I found
they'd overflowed in streams down your nightclothes.
At first we looked in silence, then the sound

of your voice saying 'This is the worst day
of my life' and 'I want to go with you'.
No tickets left. Nowhere for you to stay
if you came back with me. But then I knew

that you would return when I'd found a room
for you, a safe place for us to be in.
A flower opens inside me as I search
for a home for us. Soon, Miriam, soon.

At the beginning of this chapter I said that poetry is the writing form that is nearest to music and nearest to dance. What it also does is *strain towards silence*. It is the strongest form of written expression, evoking powerful feeling in few words, taking the reader into her deepest fears, longings and ecstasies. Emily Dickinson expressed it wonderfully:

> After great pain, a formal feeling comes –
> The Nerves sit ceremonious, like Tombs –
> The stiff Heart questions was it He, that bore
> And Yesterday, or Centuries before?
>
> The Feet, mechanical, go round –
> Of Ground, of Air or Ought –
> A Wooden way
> Regardless grown,
> A Quartz contentment, like a stone –
>
> This is the Hour of Lead –
> Remembered, if outlived,
> As Freezing persons, recollect the Snow –
> First – Chill – then Stupor – then the letting go –

The final aim of the poem is to take readers into their own silence, to bring them to rest, a state of alert yet relaxed attention, to meditate on the event, thought, feeling that the poem has placed before them. And this has to be true for the poet also: when you have allowed this final poem, the *rubaiyat*, to take you into celebration and joy, you must stop, rest, cease thinking. The work for your next poem begins in silence in the deep mysteries of your own mind. Let the gods do their work now. Sit still.

11 Preparing your Poems for Performance and Publication

In this chapter I'm going to work with you to strengthen your poems, both on the page and in performance, to find ways of reaching the essence of each poem so that it will release its full power when it is read, recited or performed, and also when it privately addresses your reader from the page.

If you've been working your way through the exercises in this book, or working steadily on poems for a year or more, you'll probably have about 12 poems by now. People write at different rates, but seem to average about one a month, if they're lucky. I'd like you to choose six of these to get ready to send out and perform. Six, because poetry magazine editors like you to send that number so they can get a sense of the variety of your work, and also because, when you get a slot at a poetry venue, six poems will enable you to showcase your work for about 15 minutes, which is a good time limit for new work. People can only concentrate for about 20 minutes, so six poems gives you time to introduce yourself, introduce and read or recite the poems, feel the response of the audience and then retire, leaving them wanting more. That's the plan, anyway!

This is a wonderful moment in your writing life, and you'll probably be feeling excited and nervous about it. You're coming out as a poet, going public, bringing your talent and your work out into the open. This is the time to remember what Jane Eyre said to the dreadful Mr Brocklehurst: 'I must stay in good health, sir, and not die.' You need to keep your health and your nerve as you move your poems from your notebook out into the wide dangerous world.

Because nobody is waiting eagerly for your work. Poetry magazine editors receive hundreds of submissions every week, and poetry audiences have heard a lot of awful poems from attention-hungry poets. They've heard it all before and they won't welcome you with open arms. They'll read or listen to your poems sceptically, critically, even suspiciously, as they should do. Who is this new person who thinks they have something to say? Well, who are you? What do you have to say? This is where your six best poems come in, to answer these questions from a world that doesn't, yet, care about your writing.

Put between 10–15 of your poems on the floor, or stick them on the walls. Walk around them. Read them. Use the Emily Dickenson test: which ones make you shiver a little, as if a voice inside the poem is awakening something inside you? There may be nothing new under the sun, but there are many ways of writing about all this old subsolar stuff, and some ways which will make people sit up and pay attention more than others. Which of your poems makes you sit up more alertly?

You may want to enlist the help of a fellow poet at this point – someone who's writing seriously, as you are, and whose judgement you trust. Many poets send their work to one another for comments and feedback. You don't have to take on everything they say, but their comments will let you know what the poem means to them and the effect it has. You'll find out from their response whether the poem carried the meaning you wanted and had the impact you intended. At the very least, it's a sanity check: am I saying what I think I'm saying?

When you've chosen your six poems, read them through again carefully. What do they tell you about your central concerns as a writer? Do they tell you that you're writing poems about nature, or poems that explore the nature of sexuality? Mystical poems or comical poems? And what kind of poems are they? Poems to be read and digested slowly? Or accessible poems that lend themselves easily to performance, poems with punch and kick that do the work for the audience and aim for an instant response? Your aim here is to see your poems from the outside, as if you were the person introducing yourself at a poetry reading, or writing the blurb on a collection of your poems. It enables you to step beyond the poems and see them as others might see them. This will give you your second glimpse into how completely you are communicating the ideas, feelings and states of being in your writing.

The integrating power of metaphor

The next aspect to look at is metaphor, which is so central a part of language that we're often not aware that we're using it. But if your metaphors are strong, they will hold your poems together with firm but delicate threads and form bridges between the world of your poem and all the other worlds to which it alludes or makes reference.

Metaphors also electrify an audience, so if you're preparing for a performance of your work, you can rely on your metaphors to create a sense of surprise and excitement in the room that will increase your audience's capacity to listen. Remember what Melquiadez said in *A Hundred Years of Solitude*: 'Things have a life of their own. It's simply a matter of waking up their souls.' Because metaphor forms a bridge between your literal subject and other things with which it is metaphorically connected, it enables your audience to see into the soul of your subject, waking it up, bringing it to life in a way that will make them shiver with recognition and surprise. This is the state that you want your listeners to be in: they weren't expecting you to make the metaphorical connection that you did, but once you made it, they felt the satisfaction of recognition. This is the great gift of metaphor: it provides excitement and fulfillment almost simultaneously.

Schools often try to teach children, in rather mechanical ways, to make similes and metaphors. The *Sun* newspaper gathered some together that had been written in exams by 16-year-olds. Here are a few of them:

> He was as lame as a duck. Not the metaphorical lame duck either, but a real duck that was actually lame. Maybe from stepping on a landmine or something.

> She grew on him like she was a colony of E coli and he was British beef at room temperature.

> He was deeply in love. When she spoke, he thought he heard bells, as if she were a dustcart reversing.

> She caught your eye like one of those pointy hook latches that used to dangle from doors and would fly up whenever you banged the door open again.

> Her voice had that tense, grating quality, like a first-generation thermal paper fax machine that needed a band tightened.

Most of these contain the giveaway word 'like', which indicates that the writers are struggling to find comparisons with their subject rather than seeking to move it into new territory. They may make you laugh, partly because it's clear that the writers are making fun of a teaching system that's made them learn simile and metaphor as though they were learning their times tables, but they don't make you shiver with the feeling that you've taken some new knowledge into your body.

Take a look at this one though:

> Memory can change the shape of a room.
> 'Oleander', in Eilis Ni Dhuibhne's collection of short stories, *The Pale Gold of Alaska*

It brings together an abstract noun, memory, and a concrete one, room, in a way that reminds us of the transformative power of memory, the way, when the present has moved into the past, which it does with every breath we take, that we can no longer hold it still. We couldn't hold it still when it was present, so many forces being at work to make the present what it is. But once, with one breath, it has moved into the past, the power of our unconscious begins to change it. It moves into the realm of memory, for which the ancient Greek word is *Mnemosyne*, who was the mother of the Muses. We could say, then, that when the present moves into the past, it moves into the realm of art. We can make stories out of it, paintings, plays. Or poems. It's past. We can't change it, or intervene in it. It's gone. All we can do is tell it in our own way.

Eilis Ni Dhuibhne has conveyed all of this and more in her brief metaphor. And, although it appeared in a story, this joining of abstractions with concretions is exactly what we do to take our poems into areas we don't yet know about, to make 'raids on the inarticulate' as T. S. Eliot put it, or 'chaos out of cosmos' as D. H. Lawrence did. We aim for primordial knowing, trying to find words for what was wordless before, using twilight language, dusky, feeling our way in the half-dark, between objects that are solid and feelings and ideas that are fluid. We ask the solid words, room, for example, to help us with the abstract ones, like memory. This is why metaphors can be so powerful and why, when they work, they make us tremble.

There's a scene in the film *Il Postino* where the postman is sitting on the beach with Pablo Neruda. The poet has been explaining metaphor to the postman so he can woo the seemingly unattainable Beatrice.

When Beatrice falls for the 'Your eyes are ... your lips are ... your breasts are ...' malarkey, the postman begins to ponder the immense power of metaphor and, with a troubled look on his face, he asks Neruda, 'Is everything a metaphor for everything else?' It's now Neruda's turn to look troubled, and he replies 'I'm going for a swim now, but I'll give you my answer when I come out.' He never does reveal the answer, so we leave the cinema none the wiser, but I can tell you now, after wrestling with the question since then, that the answer is yes. Everything is a metaphor for everything else, because it's all linked, by the finest skein, together.

The word metaphor means 'to stretch over'. It stretches over to turn a powerful light on something that was caught previously in the darkness of abstraction. It gives a body and illumination to what was obscure and abstract. Nietzsche said that writers invariably lie, because they're always searching for stronger and stronger metaphors. But a metaphor isn't a lie. It doesn't tell the literal truth, but tells the truth of the imagination, which causes the literal truth to resonate with other truths in a web of connections.

Scott Fitzgerald wrote: 'I lost my capacity for hope in the little roads that led to Zelda's sanatorium.' Literally, that's a lie. You can't lose hope like you lose a sweet wrapper in the road. But metaphorically, it is the truth. The little roads create a sense of a lost soul trying to find its way. They reveal the despair of one writer who has stifled the possible gifts of another.

But Nietzsche was right in ascribing centrality to metaphor, because it's what wakes up our writing, makes it come to life. In the poem 'Unpredicted' by John Heath-Stubbs, the poet sets a dejected, sorry-for-himself scene, and then overturns it with the wonderful lines:

> One night the unpredictable came and
> Lay in my arms.

I was reading that poem on the tube, staring blankly up at it, and when I came to that line a bolt of pleasure shot through me (a bit of a cliché, but there's another metaphor). He's taken the abstract adjective 'unpredictable' and given it a body – and there she is, lying in his arms, changing everything.

In a poetry group, one writer sent a fizz around the room (metaphor) by describing his girlfriend's ear as 'a lightbulb, South

America', drawing together a visual image of the light that passes through the fine skin of the ear and the shape of newfound land that denotes a beloved discovery. His girlfriend became both the light and the new world. That's what metaphor can do for you.

Metaphors are everywhere, enlivening and enriching all language. Here are two from the football magazine *eleven:*

> Sol Campbell might be something of a rock in the centre of the back line in the same way that a road block obstructs traffic. Rio Ferdinand is the policeman who pulls them over and asks the questions – and lets them go having confiscated their ball.
>
> Mike Collett

I think the main reason metaphor is so important for poets lies in its function as transformation: poems are a present-day echo of ancient initiations that involved a change from one state to another – from child to adult, from maiden to mother, worker to elder, living to dying. Poems are still our main religious expressions, our link with the animal and spirit realms. They show us that we are both more and less than human, that we're part of the cosmos and part of the chaos, and that everything is a part of everything else.

The 'so what?' test

Metaphor conjoins the language of instrumentality (rooms, the things we use, the way we make our way through the world) with the language of transcendence (memory, dreams, the things that defy time or seem to take place outside time: all strong feelings are included here). It is metaphor that enables poems to pass the 'so what?' test – if we merely relate what happened in our poems, the jaded reader or listener might simply shrug their shoulders and think, so what?

Tennyson wrote a long poem called 'In Memoriam' in honour of his friend Arthur Hallam, who died young. So, your friend died young. So what? It happens. Tennyson takes us beyond this compassion fatigue by using his friend's death to investigate his own feelings about death, faith and what, if anything, might lie beyond the grave. He uses the metaphor of Lazarus, the man whom Jesus raised from the dead, to explore his uncertainties, and, when the poem was published, his words so moved his readers that he was no longer a minor poet, but the nation's best-loved, and the poet laureate to boot.

Moments of recognition

Homer, or someone very much like him, wrote two long poems about warfare and returning home from war. Wars happen. People fight. Some get killed, some get home. So what? Homer's gift enabled him to take actual physical details and give them the resonance of metaphor while still retaining their physical reality. In a famous scene in *The Odyssey*, Odysseus has finally managed to get back to Ithaca, his home, but has not yet been recognised by anybody. Everything depends on his being known by his family so he can boot out the suitors who are plaguing Penelope, his wife, move in with her again and reoccupy his land. Two moments of recognition enable this to happen, and, in each, a powerful image emerges that radiates backwards through the poem with the integrating force of metaphor.

The first is Odysseus's scar. After ten years at war and ten years trying to get back, he doesn't look much like the Odysseus they all knew and loved. All he has is his scar to show that he is indeed who he says he is. And this scar comes to stand for identity, continuity, bodily vulnerability and the power of those who love us to see who we really are even though we've been transformed through time, adventure and suffering. The scar is his first password back to his former life.

The second is the bed in his house. Penelope asks him to move it and he tells her it can't be moved, because he's the only person who knows that it's carved from a rooted tree. The bed is his way back to his wife. His recognition of the uniqueness of the bed enables her to recognise him.

The word *bed* conjures images of marriage, sex and continuity: an ordered life. It stands for safety, whereas a scar stands for danger, for cutting, for breaking the rules of order. Together, the two images can call up the whole action of *The Iliad* and *The Odyssey*: Paris's flouting of the rules of being a guest; the call to arms; the long siege of Troy and the attempts to return to the world which is no longer the same. The scar and the bed help to unify the poems, stretching backwards and forwards to give the narratives an integrity and a form.

Sometimes, people read or show me poems which, because of their subject matter, should move me to tears. They may be about the poet's own experience of abuse as a child or as a sexual partner. They may be about a murder in the poet's family, or some other form of bereavement. I listen or read with close attention because I know how much hangs on the poem for the writer. But if the poem doesn't move me through its language, its rhythm, its tune, its timbre and texture, then those two words start to nag at the back of my mind. So what? How do you get beyond them? How do you make your poem work as a poem, rather than purely an expression of powerful feeling? How do you make your reader or your listener experience the feelings that your poem is trying to call up?

Consider these lines from the late poem 'Why should not old men be mad?' by W. B. Yeats:

> That if their neighbours figured plain
> As though upon a lighted screen,
> No single story would they find
> Of an unbroken, happy mind,
> A finish worthy of the start.
> Young men know nothing of this sort,
> And when they know what old books tell
> And that no better can be had,
> Know why an old man should be mad.

He's writing about being driven crazy by grief. Nobody achieves what their youthful gifts promised. Beautiful girls marry idiots. Young men become old drunks. All this drives old men crazy. It's all prize 'so what?' material. And yet it's a wonderful poem. Why?

Look at the rhythm of the poem, the controlled iambic tetrameters (four iambs in every line), and the way he varies his stresses in important places ('No single story ...', 'Young men know nothing' and 'Know why an old man ...'). Look at the rhymes, the regularity of them, and yet their apparent naturalness, and the line that ends 'what old books tell', which doesn't rhyme but stands proudly on its own, because the old books are the only source of real knowledge for the poet. Look at the images, the lighted screen, the race ('a finish worth of the start') and the books: the way they join together the inner life of contemplation with the outer life of running the race and achieving one's goals. All these things combine to give the poem its persuasive, percussive force, and take it beyond an old man's moaning about things not turning out the way he wanted them to – although the poem contains that impotent griping too, which gives it another level of poignancy.

Breathing life into your metaphors

In order to invigorate your own poems, bring them to life, inspire them, you need to be easy with your own breathing. Any kind of tension causes you to breathe shallowly, from your upper chest, thus only using a fraction of your talent and your power. Breathing from deep in the abdomen enables you to fill your whole body with oxygen. You begin to think from inside your guts and leave the brain light and empty, to call up energy through your feet and up your spine. Adequate sleep, nourishing food, plenty of water, which also brings oxygen to your cells, and deep, calm breathing are the preconditions for powerful poems – the preconditions, too, for a powerful reading or performance of your poems.

All you have to do is to be aware of your breath. Stand, or kneel, whichever is comfortable and, with your six poems around you, just breathe. Feel the breath entering your nose and passing down into your lungs, your diaphragm and your abdomen. Then, on the out breath, pull your abdomen in and feel it empty out through all your organs. When you are empty, pause a moment. This is the time of stillness, before the next breath occurs. It is a precursor to the time when we will be free of our bodies, so enjoy the freedom it brings before you begin the next breath.

You may find that the air is entering more easily through one nostril than the other. To balance the breath, simply think about the other nostril, the less open one. Whichever part of our body we focus our attention on, blood and oxygen go there, regulating and balancing it. When you know this, you can use it as a powerful technique for calming and healing any part of you that is out of harmony with the rest. After about ten breaths you'll find that you're breathing in a relaxed, balanced way. Continue doing this for five minutes. Trust me. This is not a waste of time.

At first, breathing and doing nothing else, many images will crowd into your mind. Things to do, longings, remorse about stuff you've not done, old guilts about the past and panics about the future. Let them come. It's just your ego, that knot of neuroses, desires and regrets, that is rooted in the past and the future, neither of which you can do anything about, trying to distract you from the present moment, trying to prevent you from really being present.

Only by being present, in the writing and revising of your poems, and present too in their performance, can you give your poems the attention they need. So give yourself five minutes to let go of every-thing else first. Then approach them one by one.

You've already been present once, in the making of them, when the poem first came to you, seemingly out of nowhere perhaps, or from a long-hidden memory. So it's already achieved its first expression. It exists in the world. Now you need to look at it as an object in itself. It's no longer a part of you, because, by writing it, you've made it stand alone, to make its own way in the world, creating responses and effects that are its own, no longer yours.

In one poem Yeats asked 'Did that play of mine/Send out some men the English shot?' Works of art have (especially in revolutionary times, but not only then) incredibly strong effects in the world. Be aware of this. Your poems are not nothing. They are springs, catalysts, which will move in the world in their own way once they've achieved their full power. To enable them to do this you must stand back and see them as separate. That's why you have them around you on the floor or on the walls: things in themselves that are beginning the process of becoming things *for* themselves. The process of moving from becoming to being.

Approach each of the poems in turn, first for metaphor. As you look at each poem, underline any image, symbol or trope (figurative lan-guage) that takes it beyond itself and causes it to stretch over into other aspects of the world. Write these images down so that they stand alone on separate sheets of paper. Look at them. Breathe. Relax. Are these images alive? Do they make you feel that you are involved in a conversation with living, breathing things?

If you are unconvinced by any of them, examine their nouns and their verbs. Is there a balance between abstract and concrete nouns? 'She knows it in the bleak orphanage that her heart has suddenly become' has one pronoun, 'She', one concrete noun, 'bleak orphan-age', and one abstract noun, 'her heart'. You can see that, as with 'Memory can change the shape of a room', the abstract noun expands and transforms the meaning of the concrete, and vice versa. Are your nouns doing this work of transformation? If not, try making one of them more specific, perhaps by adding an adjective, the way that here we have 'bleak orphanage' instead of just 'orphanage'. If you are still unsatisfied, look at the verbs that hold your metaphors together. Are they all 'is' and 'are'? If so, they could be holding your metaphors in a rather passive state. Try imagining what your nouns might be doing to one another, and make your verbs more active accordingly.

Take a look now at this poem by the poet and novelist Martina Evans:

> For I will consider My Cat Eileen Murphy
> For I am annoyed with her.
> For she doesn't kiss My Cat Alice in kindness.
> For she bullies Alice and pushes her off high walls.
> For she is only interested in her own coat.
> For she sucks up to visitors and ignores me.
> For she strikes the centre of my back to wake me if she thinks there is a hope of tuna.
> For Alice cringes when she approaches.
> For she roars for her food and reprimands me.
> For her hairs cause too much work with the hoover and the roll of sellotape.
> For she will always desert me for patches of sunlight.
> For she runs away from me in front of the neighbours.
> For she clings to my lap when she is only looking for a heat-up.
> For her colours; soft grey, fawn, shining white, honey, sand, gold, black and peach laugh in the face of designers and manufacturers.
> For she sought out Liadain when Liadain was very sad and pressed herself against Liadain's side in such way that tenderness could not be mistaken.
> For she has the outline of a tiara marked out on the top of her head.
> For the length and strength of her whiskers are the proof of God's bounty.
> For we know that she doesn't pretend.
> For she is a striped stravaganza with a tiara on her head.
> For she gives a damn.

This 'For I will consider' poem is a response to the eighteenth-century poet Christopher Smart's 'For I will consider my cat Geoffrey', which itself is full of Smart's own marvellous, idiosyncratic love of his maker and all creatures. Martina Evans' poem works on one level, literally, as an exploration of the vices and virtues of her cat, and on another, metaphorically, as a contemplation of the qualities of cunning and survival, tenderness and compassion that human beings share with cats. Eileen Murphy really exists in the poem, but she also exists as a trope, to enable us to explore these seemingly contradictory qualities with the poet.

Look at the verbs in the poem. They move, don't they? Not one of them is static, so they cause us to consider the cat and her qualities from many angles. We feel her sucking up to us, stretch out with her in patches of sunlight, watch her bullying the weaker cat, pushing her off high walls. It's all specific and funny, and you can see how the verbs do a lot of the work.

Now look at the verbs in your own metaphors again and see how much more you can make them do for you. Make them work. Make them play. Make them roll around in the mud with your nouns.

Making your poems dance and sing

Although many contemporary poems don't abide by any strict metre, you can gain a deeper insight into how they work by marking their strong and weak beats. Like this:

For she will always desert me for patches of sunlight

For she runs away from me in front of the neighbours.

For she clings to my lap when she is only looking for a heat-up.

In these lines you can see a preponderance of anapaests, two weak beats followed by a strong one. It's a rollicking, rising metre which causes the energy of each line to build up. And yet the lines tend to end on a weak beat, a falling-off, which helps to sustain the bathos, the sublime-to-the-ridiculous mood and tone of the poem.

When your own poems first came to you, you may not have been aware of the rhythms in which they were making themselves known. That's as it should be. The poem comes, we don't always know how. But you can make yourself aware of the rhythms now, by going through each of them, marking the strong beats and the weak beats. Do the strong beats fall where you want them to? You're working with the rhythms of everyday speech, but poetry offers you the opportunity to turn seemingly everyday words into conjunctions and constellations that make the reader or listener aware of the ghost of a dance, a dirge or a march within apparently ordinary words and phrases. If you mark the rhythm of your poem, you'll learn more about what it is trying to tell you. Walking around the landscape of the poem according to the poem's own rhythm, you will find that different nouns, verbs, adjectives, adverbs and prepositions may come to you which are more faithful to the rhythm the poem wants.

And, when you've done all this, dance out your poems. Feel the rhythm of each poem in your feet and in your whole body. That way you bring them inside you again.

Now let's look at the poem's tune. Although most poems are no longer sung, they do nevertheless each have their own melody. Look at each one until it reveals its melody to you. Do the high notes correspond to the strong beats of the rhythm, or do they syncopate, working against each other like blues or jazz? Where are the low notes? What do they tell you about the fundamental, deep, perhaps hidden forces in the poem? When the melody is clear to you, sing your poem out loud. This will give you a clear sense of where to raise and lower your voice when you are performing.

The *timbre* of your poem is its quality of sound. Is it a full orchestra or a single flute? A massed choir or a drum? Does it possess a quiet, private voice, speaking to the reader confidingly or secretly, or is it an out-in-the-square, public, ranting or showing-off voice? You can alter the timbre, as you can change the dynamics, the loudness or softness of a poem, to suddenly bring the reader very close or make him or her a part of the crowd. Compare the timbre of these lines from Benjamin Zephaniah's 'Bought and Sold' with Martina Evans' poem:

> The ancestors would turn in graves
> These poor black folk that once were slaves
>   would wonder
> How our souls were sold
> And check our strategies.
> The empire strikes back and waves
> Tamed warriors bow on parades
> When they have done what they've been told
> They get their OBEs.
>
> Don't take my word, go check the verse
> cause every laureate gets worse ...

They couldn't be more different, could they? There's nothing soft or stretching about these lines. They get their quality of sound and their dynamics from the driving force of protest and anger, a force that has carried writing, when it's been needed, from that furious Greek play

The Trojan Women to Osip Mandelstam's poem about Stalin. And now this marvellous attack on a society that likes to subdue its critics by stuffing their mouths with gold and honours.

Look back again at your own poems. Are there feelings hidden in them that could do with being brought out? Don't be shy. You can strengthen your voice by letting it be loud and angry when it wants to be. If you find that you have one of these poems, one you've sometimes been ashamed of, or thought you should take out behind the barn and shoot, bring it out now. You may find a quality there, something strong enough to end a performance with.

Strengthening your physical voice

The *Observer* magazine's barefoot doctor quotes his old friend as saying: 'Your voice is the messenger of the gods, boy – use it well!' and offers various simple exercises for developing what the Taoists call a 'virtuous voice'.

The first is for *flexibility*. This will give your voice variety, and enable you to give the high notes and the low notes of your poems their full flavour. Start with the sound 'aaaah', and slide with it from the highest note you can reach down to the lowest. Then do the same with 'eeyoh', starting very high with the 'eeee' sound and going as low as you can with 'yoh'. Do this three times each day during the week before a performance.

Now we'll work on *resonance*, which is your voice's ability to cause vibrations as you speak. These vibrations are made in your skull and you can develop them into a more pleasing music by practising these sounds: 'mmmm' to vibrate the front of your face, 'nnnn' to vibrate your nasal cavity, and 'nnnng' to vibrate the back of the skull. The barefoot doctor says that this is also a great way to clear blocked sinuses or a hangover head!

You can learn to *project* your voice more effectively by choosing a note and chanting it for as long as your breath lasts, picturing your voice hitting a spot on the wall opposite. Relax your abdomen while you're doing this, enabling 'the curve of happiness' to happen to your belly. When you do this as performance, you'll be making eye contact with different members of the audience, but sending your voice beyond them to the back wall, so it bounces back and enfolds the whole audience with the sound of your words.

It will also help your performance if you can improve the *muscularity* of your voice. This means being able to form strong consonants which can contain your vowels and give your poems the clarity and definition they deserve. Take a deep breath and go through the alphabet like this: ba, ba, ba, ca, ca, ca, da, da, da, – all the way through, using any rhythm you like. Try dancing it again, to develop the muscularity of your whole body as well as the muscles in your throat.

Once you've practised all these exercises, read or recite your poems in an empty room, and time them, so you know exactly how long your performance will take.

Angela Dove is a well-known poet and MC for poetry events in London. She's been hosting live poetry at different venues for about ten years, so she knows all the pitfalls and how to avoid them. To help with all the details of performance, here are Angela's 'nineteen ways to be a good poetry performer':

1. Get as much advance information about the event and venue as you can. Do a 'recce' beforehand, and turn up at least 30 minutes before the event starts. Never assume anything in terms of lighting, sound, seating and so on. Possibly it won't be there!

2. Select the poems carefully for the time you have been allotted. Don't be tempted to overrun. Leave them wanting more. Rehearse at home with a clock. Include time for an introduction and links. Keep a couple of extra poems up your sleeve. Wear a watch at the event. Don't rely on the MC to time you. It's not his/her job.

3. Have a performance copy of your poems. Put the poems in a simple folder in the right order. Have copies in a fairly large font, in bold unless you have brilliant eyesight, as venue lighting is often poor. Audiences don't want to see poets shuffling through papers.

4. Memorise your poems if you are confident, but nerves can affect memory, so have the printed copy with you anyway. Don't attempt it unless you are really sure you can pull it off.

5. Start and finish with your best work. It's like a good meal – a tempting starter and a memorable dessert work wonders.

6. What you wear affects you and the audience. Feel confident physically. Wear what you feel good in. Venues can be hot and stuffy. Don't overdress.

7. Dutch courage: only you know how alcohol affects you. If in any doubt, leave it for the post-performance chill-out time.

8. Water should be provided for performers, but take a bottle anyway. Nerves dry up the mouth, and it's OK to have a drink of water between poems.

9. If the MC introduces you, thank him/her. If not, say who you are, and 'good evening/hello', like a good host at a party. It's good to place your work in context, but don't be tempted to give the audience your personal biography. They are here for your poems, so use your time well.

10. Don't apologise. Avoid introducing a poem with 'This is unfinished, a rather depressing poem. The next poem probably won't work. I'm afraid this is yet another poem about my father …' and so on. Even if you are nervous, don't tell the audience. If you act confidently, it will carry you through.

11. Take your time. These poems may have taken you weeks to write. Honour that now and allow the audience to take them in.

12. Less is more. A ten-minute set is adequate time to communicate your work to an audience who will possibly have been listening to a couple of sets before yours, and more after.

13. Breath is the key to spoken word performance. When you rehearse, identify and practise breathing points in the poems. The breath supports your voice. If your voice feels weak, pause, take a deep breath from the diaphragm, and continue.

14. If you are faced with a microphone, try and get a chance to do a quick sound check before the event starts. If you are not comfortable with the microphone, you can always choose not to use it.

15. Many a good poem is lost simply because the audience can't hear it. If in doubt after you introduce yourself, ask if people can hear, then adjust accordingly. Pitch your voice to an imaginary friend standing right at the centre back of the venue.

16. At the start, make eye contact with your audience, and find opportunities to do this as you read. It's a powerful way of establishing communication, and that's what readings are all about.

17. If you are reading with other poets, listen carefully to their poems. There may be great opportunities to link their work with your own, and it makes added value for the audience.

18. Acknowledge applause. It's your chance to get something back. Don't rush off the platform. Smile, enjoy it and say thanks.

19. Afterwards try to find time to thank your event organiser and fellow poets. They also have worked hard to make it a success.

Your poetry performance will reveal a great deal to you. You'll find that some of your poems command a richer quality of attention than others. It may sound strange, but you can gauge this by listening to the quality of silence that greets your poems. Sometimes the room is hushed, the audience's breath bated, and you can hear your words sinking slowly into your listeners' minds. Then you know that you have a good one, a poem you can send out to a poetry or arts magazine. On the other hand, there may be a light movement, or even just a feeling of distraction in the air. Then you know that you haven't got your audience with you, and that this particular poem may well need more work.

Sending out your poems

When you reach the point when you want to see your work in print, you should begin to research the poetry magazine market. The National Poetry Library will enable you to obtain the names and addresses of these. Send away for one magazine at a time. Read it through to get a sense of the kinds of poems the editor(s) like to accept. Think, too, about whether you like the magazine. If you don't, if the work in it feels alien to you, don't bother with it. You want to appear in a magazine that you like and admire.

When you've chosen which one you want to send to, prepare fair copies of your six poems, and send them with a letter to the editors. Your letter can be short, simply telling them the titles of the poems you're sending, but it can also include details of any previous publications, performances or prizes in poetry competitions. We like to think that the poems will stand on their own, and in the long run they will, but I know, from opening the many poems that arrived every day for *Ambit* magazine, that if a poet had some form, it would give the poems an edge, and I would usually glance curiously at them before filing them away to be looked at in their turn. And if I liked them, I would put them on the editor's desk, so they'd jump the long queue to be seen.

Don't forget a stamped addressed envelope! They'll throw your poems away if you don't include one.

All you need now is the patience and determination to weather the many rejections you may receive before your work is accepted. Don't give up. Remember what I said at the beginning of this chapter, that you're creating your own audience. It doesn't exist yet, but it will.

In the Further Reading section at the back of this book, I've listed some of the poetry magazines I like and find interesting. But remember that editors get tired and hand the work over to another editor. You may find that the address has changed, so it's as well to check the current state of play on the magazine's website. You'll be able to get hold of these by logging on to the National Poetry Library's magazines website, which I've also listed at the back. I've also included some American poetry magazines.

I advise poets to send six poems so the editor can get a taste of the different tones and aspects of your work. They sometimes like a poem you don't think much of, that you've just thrown in at the last minute. There's no accounting for taste. One magazine may like funny poems, or poems of a sexual nature. Another may publish more spiritual poems. You'll discover what the editors like by reading their publications. The late editor of *The London Magazine*, Alan Ross, was once asked what his tastes were in poetry. He said: 'Women, India and cricket.' If a poem arrived on his desk containing any or all of these themes, he would read it with great interest. Alan Ross died and Sebastian Barker took over the editorship of *The London Magazine*, and when you look at the magazine now you'll see that the writers and their themes are quite different. So keep up to date with your reading.

Don't lose heart, and don't let your spirits be crushed. Poets are the artists most likely to succumb to mental illness and even suicide. If there's any danger of this, get all the help you can, from friends, family, therapists and doctors. Sometimes you may not think the world wants your work, but it does. The world needs poems – always has, always will.

12   Love Writing

Conversation between men and women has barely begun
Theodore Zeldin, An Intimate History of Humanity

Playing means giving oneself temporary freedom from duty and necessity, voluntarily taking risks and being excited because one does not know the outcome; 'pretending' is self-conscious delight in alternative possibilities, and appreciation of the fact that no victory is final. Is it an accident that the verb to win derives from the Indo-European root *wen*, to desire, and the verb to lose from the root *los*, to set free? Can playing at winning and losing be an apprenticeship in freedom? The Spanish to win, *ganar*, derives from the Gothic *ganari*, to covet, while *perder* (to lose) comes from the Latin *perdere*, which originally meant to give completely. The courtly lover who did not want to possess his ideal, who played to lose, discovered that whereas business and war were prosaically about possession, in love it was play that mattered most. Being willing to play is one of the conditions of creativity. Love, far from being a distraction from creativity, is a branch of it.

Ibid., p. 89

Zeldin's thoughts about love and play can easily be seen as a way of thinking about writing, too. We give ourselves completely to it, we play to lose, we lose ourselves, we use ourselves and our time in our ardour to write, we ache sometimes when some other duty prevents us from performing this primary duty to ourselves:

You write: *Three and a half weeks lost from writing …*
I think of the word *protection*
who it is we try to protect and why

'Coast to Coast' in Adrienne Rich,
A Wild Patience Has Taken Me This Far

And at some time in our lives, we end up writing about love, because love is as inescapable as breathing. We breathe to live, and if we are to be fully alive, we have to love. If C. S. Lewis is right when he says that the aim of creation is to increase joy, then love is the power-house, the driving force behind that increase. We experience joy when we love and when we are loved, but love involves great risk, and unreturned or only partially returned love are only two of the risks we take when we begin to love:

> What makes love unusual among the emotions is the human inability to do without it ... Only love is both completely indispensable to the func-tioning of human society and a source of the fullest satisfaction known to human beings – despite the fact that loving or being loved often pro-duces as much pain as it does pleasure. For love is always subject to frustration and rejection, and commonly bound together with such dangerous emotions as jealousy, hate, and fear. But this fact merely emphasizes that the beloved can be valued as having inherent worth even when giving pain and not simply when giving pleasure.
>
> Robert Brown, *Analyzing Love*, pp. 126–7

I think that writers write about love out of its absence. When it is there, there is fullness. When it is gone, for a little while or for good, we conjure it back in our writing. This again is the magic of writing: nothing need ever be completely lost, because we give it back to our-selves when we find the words to say it.

But we are sometimes rendered speechless by all that's gone before. Dante's *Divine Comedy*, Shakespeare's sonnets, Toni Morrison's *Beloved*, Isabel Allende's *Paula*: what else is there to say? And as well as the real stuff there's the garbage, pulp fiction fantasies that churn out the same old formulae that we all know don't work. These can make us despair of anything new ever happening, because they seem designed to keep their readers in outworn ways of thinking and feeling, fearful of experimentation, using fiction as a compensation for what isn't coming into being in their own lives, rather than as a guide and liberator, suggesting new possibilities, new combinations, new opportunities.

So what I want to do in this chapter is to take you on a Cook's tour of some of the things I've read about love. My choice of reading is random and at times idiosyncratic – I've simply followed my nose – but I'm indebted for help with thinking about the texts to writing groups at the City Lit, who generously and bravely shared their insights with me and never shied away from any question, however personal. Always remember that conversation is one of the writer's best tools. We learn by talking and listening. New possibilities of plot, character, internal and external weather emerge from talking to friends. When Ben Elton was questioned on how he could deliver such accurate comedy about women, he answered 'I ask them things'.

My aim here is to show that people have written about love in many different ways, that people think of love according to how they live. What's possible at one time is taboo at another. Love changes, grows or goes around according to people's particular conditions of existence. Colin Turnbull's *The Mountain People* is a study of the Ik, a people so dispossessed of their land and means of livelihood that they seemed to have no love, either between adults or between adults and children. This too, devastating as it is, is possible. But circumstances of extreme hardship and cruelty usually contain some evidence of the persistence of love. It was there in the concentration camps, where sometimes people could still make the leap of putting themselves in someone else's shoes and so offer compassion and comfort even when they were close to death themselves. The forms of love depend on where and when we find it.

But let's begin with an attempt at definition. What is love? Where did it come from? An account I enjoy immensely is Plato's (but remember you will find others. Fish around for those that suit your own purposes). In his *Symposium*, Plato writes about Socrates (who was condemned to death by the Athenian state in 399 BC for asking too many questions) and his visit to Diotima, the wise woman of Mantineia, to find out about the nature of love. This is what she told him about the birth of love:

> On the birthday of Aphrodite there was a feast of the gods, at which the god Poros or Plenty, who is the son of Metis or Discretion, was one of the guests. When the feast was over, Penia or Poverty, as the manner is on such occasions, came about the doors to beg. Now Plenty, who was the worse for nectar (there was no wine in those days), went into the garden of Zeus and fell into a heavy sleep; and Poverty, considering her own straitened circumstances, plotted to have a child by him, and accordingly she lay down at his side and conceived Love, who partly because he is a lover of the beautiful, and also because he was born on her birthday, is her follower and attendant. And as his parentage is, so also are his fortunes. In the first place he is always poor, and anything but tender and fair, as the many imagine him; and he is rough and

squalid, and has no shoes, nor a house to dwell in; on the bare earth exposed he lies under the open heaven, in the streets, or at the doors of houses, taking his rest; and like his mother he is always in distress. Like his father too, whom he also partly resembles, he is always plotting against the fair and the good; he is bold, enterprising, strong, a mighty hunter, always weaving some intrigue or other, keen on the pursuit of wisdom, fertile in resources; a philosopher at all times, terrible as an enchanter, sorcerer, sophist. He is by nature neither mortal or immortal, but alive and flourishing at one moment when he is in plenty, and dead at another moment, and again alive by reason of his father's nature. But that which is always flowing in is always flowing out, and so he is never in want and never in wealth; and, further, he is in a mean between ignorance and knowledge … for wisdom is a most beautiful thing, and Love is of the beautiful; and therefore Love is also a philosopher or lover of wisdom, and being a Lover of wisdom is in a mean between the wise and the ignorant. And of this too his birth is the cause; for his father is wealthy and wise, and his mother poor and foolish. Such, my dear Socrates, is the nature of the spirit Love. The error in your conception of him was very natural, and as I imagine from what you say, has arisen out of a confusion of love and the beloved, which made you think that love was all beautiful, and delicate, and perfect, and blessed; but the principle of love is of another nature, and is such as I have described.

Plato, *Symposium*, pp. 257–9

Think what fun it might be to write your own version of this story. Imagine the scene: some princess-type is throwing a birthday party for herself. Some of the beautiful people are there, and one of the cutest is this man Paulus with fine teeth who's made it in the city. Veuve Cliquot flows. Around midnight the princess's scrawny cousin, Beany, slopes in. She's given the best years of her life to social work, been made redundant, and is not in good shape. What's more, her biological clock is doing its stuff and she's had it with looking out for other people. She wants a little something for herself. When she takes her jacket to the bedroom she finds Paulus snoozing away on the soft, expensive coats. She bends down and begins to stroke him.

Try it. What kind of baby would they have? What would Beany do? Would she tell Paulus she was pregnant, or hoard the little love all to herself? What part would Paulus play? Would he use some of the money he's made in futures to bankroll his son's education (or is

Loveday a daughter?) or will the child have to watch out for himself, street-urchin-wise?

All the big ideas are in this one: sexual conflict, money, transgression, the bright hope for the future. You could make anything out of it, from a fable to a novel. Think about it. Try it.

Plato's wise woman makes it clear that love is double-sided: fierce and tender, cruel and gentle, empty and beautiful. She argues that it is the beloved who is all-beautiful, not love itself. There is a story by Raymond Carver called 'What We Talk About When We Talk About Love' that has four people sitting round a table drinking gin, trying to work out whether the destructive impulse, when the lover tries to harm the beloved (in this story, out of jealousy) is also part of the feeling we call love. They don't come to any conclusion about it, they just carry on drinking the gin until it is finished, but Mel, the particularly 'peaceful' one among them, who has argued all the way through that love is mild and not violent, admits at the end of the story that he'd like to murder his ex-wife (with a swarm of bees! She's allergic to bees) because 'she's vicious'.

In Carver's story, Mel, a doctor, is married to Terri. Before Terri was with Mel she was with Ed:

> Terri said the man she lived with before she lived with Mel loved her so much he tried to kill her. Then Terri said 'He beat me up one night. He dragged me around the living room by my ankles. He kept saying "I love you, I love you, you bitch." He kept on dragging me around the living room. My head kept knocking on things.' Terri looked around the table. 'What do you do with love like that?'

When Terri left, Ed took rat poison, but it didn't kill him. He menaced Mel when he got together with Terri and threatened to kill him. Finally, he shot himself in the mouth, but that didn't kill him either. Mel, who is a doctor, was at the hospital when he was brought in. Mel resumes the story:

> 'The man lived for three days. His head swelled up to twice the size of a normal head. I'd never seen anything like it, and I hope I never do again. Terri wanted to go in and sit with him when she found out about it. We had a fight over it. I didn't think she should see him like that. I didn't think she should see him, and I still don't.'
> 'Who won the fight?' Laura said.

'I was in the room with him when he died,' Terri said. 'He never came up out of it. But I sat with him. He didn't have anyone else.'

'He was dangerous,' Mel said. 'If you call that love you can have it.'

'It was love,' Terri said. 'Sure it's abnormal in most people's eyes. But he was willing to die for it. He did die for it.'

'I sure as hell wouldn't call it love,' Mel said. 'I mean, no one knows what he did it for. I've seen a lot of suicides, and I couldn't say anyone ever knew what they did it for.'

Mel put his hands behind his neck and tilted his chair back. 'I'm not interested in that kind of love,' he said. 'If that's love, you can have it.'

Raymond Carver, 'What We Talk About
When We Talk About Love'

Well, *is* that love? Can cruelty, destructiveness and self-destructiveness ever be described as love? And how do we classify cruelty? Sexual love involves the physical penetration of one person by another. Is that cruel? Sexual love may also involve sadistic or masochistic fantasies. Are two people still loving each other when involved in imaginary scenarios of dominance and submission? The psychoanalyst Donald Winnicott said that when a man and woman have a baby, the baby is evidence that the sadism of each partner has not destroyed the other, because there is a baby, who proves that their love is sound, nourishing and positive. The baby is proof that the couple have not broken each other, and that there is something healthy at the heart of their love-making. Is love always hovering between hurt and healing, holding its own pain and its own soothing, often tipping the scales down so far on the side of destruction, that no reparation is possible? Oscar Wilde said 'each man kills the thing he loves' (*The Ballad of Reading Gaol*, I, vii). Is that true, in your own experience?

I want you to imagine this going both ways now. First, something going wrong with a connection between two people. In their book *Conscious Loving*, Gay and Kathlyn Hendricks describe the way that holes tend to open up between people who have started to love each other:

> As a result of the closeness you experience in the romance phase, unpleasant parts of your personality will begin to emerge. You learned certain problem feelings and patterns in earlier close relationships, and the closeness you are experiencing now is bringing them to the surface. This is inevitable: you have no choice. Meanwhile, the unpleasant parts of your partner are beginning to emerge. Later a choice point occurs, which will determine the destiny of the relationship.

They go on to list issues of trust, authority, self-esteem, long-repressed feelings and sexuality as areas of vulnerability when two people are attempting to make and keep a connection. Any one of these could create wonderful tension in a story. Try one that begins with two people having supper. A song of Morrissey's is playing. The words coming through are

> You're the one for me, Fatty,
> You're the one I really, really love
>
> Morrissey, 'You're the one for me, Fatty',
> *Your Arsenal*

and one of the two people is singing along to it, looking at the other ironically, even mockingly. The other person gets up and leaves the table. What happens next? Make this a short story, only two or three pages, which invites the reader to enter into the feelings of the person whose self-esteem and trust in the other have been punctured. Show the hole opening up. Leave it ragged and still open at the end.

Now try it the other way round. Something has happened to break the calm and trust between two people. One of them decides to heal the break. In wanting to put it right, he or she thinks back to when something similar happened in the past, when they themselves were hurt and betrayed. What did they long for, to mend it, then? Could they find that gesture and use it to approach the other? Make this one happen very slowly. Take us slowly back into the lover's memory as they search for and discover the key that might open the door. Then let the gesture of reparation occur tentatively and delicately, with the lover aware that he or she is touching a raw, wounded place, which nevertheless needs to be touched to prevent the growth of hard, resistant scar tissue.

There is a strong tradition within many cultures which holds that the sufferings of love have a refining, perfecting effect on the lover, and that the soul should embrace such suffering in order to achieve wholeness. A beautiful exploration of this theme is the story of Yusuf and Zulaykha, told in sura 12 of the Qur'an and elaborated upon by Jami, the Sufi writer and mystic. Yusuf is the Joseph of the Old Testament. He is the Lord's best beloved, the perfect man. Zulaykha falls in love with him after seeing him in a dream, seated upon a throne in a garden. 'One look at the man was enough to pierce Zulaykha's heart, sending a sharp pain through her body. Yet, it was

as if she enjoyed the pain, for she could not take her eyes off the man.'
By mistake, thinking she is marrying Yusuf, she marries the grand
vizier of Egypt, and Yusuf, sold into slavery by his brothers, arrives in
that country and is bought by Zulaykha and her husband. Zulaykha is
desperate to be with Yusuf, but he repels all her advances. 'If, in fact,
you feel as you claim,' he says to her, 'you should know that one
whose heart is given to a friend thinks no longer of herself but loses
herself in the wish of the friend. Her happiness lies in doing whatever
the friend desires – and my wish and desire is to be a servant to you
and your husband.'

The story is quite long. Zulaykha remains possessed by her love,
falling deeper and deeper into anguish. Yusuf is thrown into prison
and not released until he is thirty, when he interprets a dream
that is tormenting the pharaoh, and is himself made a grand vizier.
Zulaykha's husband dies, and she spends the last of her silver
paying for news of Yusuf. She becomes old, bent, with silver-white
hair, eyes blinded by tears, and homeless. At last she shatters the
idol she has prayed to for years and prays to God for forgiveness.
'Let my heart be healed of the wounds of regret, and let me pick a
flower from Yusuf's garden. O Pure Being Who makes a king a lowly
slave and crowns a slave with the royal crown ...'.

Yusuf then passes by, sees her, and asks who she is. She describes
what has befallen her because of her love for him, and he asks the Lord
why he didn't take her, why he allowed her to live in such suffering.
The Lord replies:

> We have not taken her, for she has within her a whole world of love for
> him whom We love. Since her love for you is unceasing, We too love her
> for your sake. Who gave you the permission to seek the death of a rose
> in Our garden and to wish for the destruction of the friend of Our
> friend? Since she is filled with tenderness for you, how could you think
> We would take her life? Her weeping eyes bear witness to her love.
> Though for a lifetime We have driven her to despair, now We will make
> her young again for you. She has given you her own precious soul; if We
> now bless her, let her be to you as your soul.

Then the Lord restores Zulaykha's beauty and gives her eyes such a
ray of truth that Yusuf is lost in them. They are united in marriage,
have many children and become 'as one'. When the Lord calls Yusuf
to him, Zulaykha dies too. The story ends with the words 'Lucky the

lovers who, in dying, breathe their last with the aroma of Union in their nostrils.'

You will notice, even in this compressed version, how the story is the prototype for what we think of as the great love stories. The lover is transformed through love, endures terrible suffering and becomes worthy of the beloved when her life seems to be over. The key seems to be humiliation: Zulaykha bears humiliation for the sake of her love, again and again, all her life. It is only God's pity which brings her humiliation to an end.

It is this humiliation I want you now to explore, this willing giving of the self into the keeping of the beloved, the other, who can protect or hurt it as they desire. Theodore Zeldin's definition of 'to lose', 'which originally meant to give completely', might help here. You will find examples of this voluntary giving all around you, from your own experience and by observing others. The amazing thing about love is that it overturns our expectations about human selfishness. I found an instance of it at my younger daughter's school. Her teacher took me aside and said 'You know Sean is in love with Miriam?' (They are nine.) I nodded, trying to look *au fait*. 'Well', she continued, 'he made a statue of her and showed it to her. I expected her to be delighted, but she was furious and she beat him. And do you know, he took the blows, almost gladly. He didn't fight back.' So you see, it starts young, this glad bearing of the wounds of love.

There is an astonishing poem which takes this much further in Seamus Heaney's collection *The Spirit Level*. Here it is:

St Kevin and the Blackbird

And then there was St Kevin and the blackbird.
The saint is kneeling, arms stretched out, inside
his cell, but the cell is narrow, so

One turned up palm is out the window, stiff
As a crossbeam, when a blackbird lands
And lays in it and settles down to nest.

Kevin feels the warm eggs, the small breast, the tucked
Neat head and claws and, finding himself linked
Into the network of eternal life,

Is moved to pity: now he must hold his hand

Like a branch out in the sun and rain for weeks
Until the young are hatched and fledged and flown.

*

And since the whole thing's imagined anyhow,
Imagine being Kevin. Which is he?
Self-forgetful or in agony all the time

From the neck on out down through his hurting forearms?
Are his fingers sleeping? Does he still feel his knees?
Or has the shut-eyed blank of underearth

Crept up through him? Is there distance in his head?
Alone and mirrored clear in love's deep river,
'To labour and not to seek reward,' he prays,

A prayer his body makes entirely
For he has forgotten self, forgotten bird
And on the riverbank forgotten the river's name.

In this poem, Kevin bears the physical hardship because he is *within love*, that sphere of beauty and danger that calls forth from us more than we imagine we're capable of giving. Here, love not only takes Kevin beyond selfish desires, but beyond the self entirely, manifestly into the 'network of eternal life'.

Try to imagine this terrain of 'beyond', where tremendous hardships, physical, emotional, spiritual, can be suffered either for the sake of the beloved or for love itself. Take your reader into the endurance. Let her feel the pain your lover is feeling.

Finally, remember that love is the engine that drives all your work. Sometimes it may seem to you that you are writing out of hate or revenge or 'I'll show them', but this stretching out that we do with our hands into the world outside, and this nurturing of the world in our hands, is akin to what St Kevin is doing: waiting patiently, with all the strength in our minds and bodies, to bring new life into being, to create the conditions in which it can be born, and calmly, humbly, to be the midwife who helps it into the world. Writing is nothing more and nothing less than this.

13   Doing your Research

When an idea comes to you, for a novel, a play or a screenplay, how do you take it from its embryo state to a place where you are ready to let it stand as a work on its own? How can you find out enough about your idea so you can feel confident about using it in your writing? Gabriel García Márquez, when speaking about *The Autumn of the Patriarch*, said that he spent ten years reading about dictators, and then forgot everything he had read while he was writing his novel. Do all writers do their research beforehand, before they begin writing? To answer these questions I spoke with some novelists and screenwriters about their ways of working. What I wanted to discover was a set of guidelines emerging from my conversations with experienced writers, guidelines to keep in mind which will help you as you begin to investigate the material for your own work, whether it's a novel or a script. Here is what I found out.

Harriet Grace

Harriet Grace is a novelist and poet whose first novel is at present with an agent. So she has reached the first stage: an agent has taken it on, but it hasn't yet found a publisher. Her novel revolves around the theme of fertility. Written in three voices, we hear the story from the points of view of Martha, a features editor on an English national newspaper, her husband, a psychoanalyst, and also a messenger on the features floor, an attractive young man who doesn't seem able to find his direction in life.

The first thing Harriet Grace needed to research was how the features department on a newspaper works, so she contacted the *Guardian* and spoke to the personal assistant to the features editor there. The PA talked through with Harriet what happens on a typical day, and invited her to come to the building so she could get to know the geography of the place. Harriet spent a day there, watching what was going on and taking in the layout of the department. She also looked at various features, and then visited the features department of the *Daily Telegraph*, on the 15th floor at Canary Wharf, to get the feel of a different kind of newspaper in a different kind of place.

In Harriet's novel, Martha and her husband are childless, and Martha wants a child, although she doesn't know where this want comes from, and doesn't entirely trust it. Harriet, therefore, needed to find out about fertility treatment. To research this, she telephoned Hammersmith hospital and spoke with an *in vitro* fertilisation counsellor, who told her that when a treatment fails, couples tend to keep trying again and again. In the novel, Martha and her husband are experiencing what's called 'unexplained infertility'. They've tried to have a child, but can't, for some unknown reason. What interested Harriet, and this is one of the main themes of the novel, is why a woman who seemed to have everything is obsessed with having a child when she doesn't really know why she wants one.

Martha's husband has to return to San Francisco because his mother has a stroke. While he is there, he thinks the marriage will not last. Meanwhile Martha, in London, is thinking she is pregnant. A little later the young man, who has become a friend of both of them, comes round one Saturday thinking they'll both be there. Martha, however, is alone, and distressed because she's discovered she's not pregnant after all.

Harriet told me that she found she had to walk around the part of London where she had the couple living, and also around San Francisco, so she could feel she was with her characters as they moved about their lives. Then she said that she has to let the characters grow inside her, has to wait until she can really hear their voice, and that this takes a lot of time.

I derived a checklist of guidelines from what Harriet told me:

1. Be clear about what you want to find out.
2. Ask people who know. Harriet found that people actively wanted to help her, and gave their time and knowledge generously.
3. Get as much written information as you can.
4. Get to know the areas you are writing about at ground level. Walk the streets. Feel the atmosphere.
5. Give your characters time to grow inside you. Feel them as people. Hear their voices.

Martina Evans

Martina Evans is an Irish novelist and poet, living in London, with three novels and two collections of poetry published. She won the Betty Trask Award for her first novel, *Midnight Feast*, has a fellowship from the Royal Literary Fund, and teaches creative writing. At present she's working on a novel with the working title *Bold O'Donohue*, set during the time of the struggle for Irish independence, between 1902 and 1920. She talked with me about the development of this novel, and also about how her third novel, *No Drinking, No Dancing, No Doctors*, came into being.

With this third novel, she told me that the image that first came to her was of a somewhat cranky man who was born in the 1930s, and that this man subsequently changed into a woman. Martina wanted to write about religion, but not directly about Catholicism. What she did, therefore, was to invent her own religion, a fierce Protestant sect that allows none of the comforts listed in her book's title.

Her inspiration also came from a memory. Before she began to work full time as a writer and a teacher, she was a radiographer in a hospital. She remembers preparing to X-ray an orthodox Jewish man who clearly found it hard to be treated by a woman, and who asked her to call in his wife to be with him. His wife entered, turned her back on him and gazed out of the window at the traffic while eating a banana. The memory of this couple, and Martina's own unease in the man's presence (she said she felt like a painted Jezebel, especially as she'd also just hennaed her hair), was the driving force in imagining the religious sect. She also said that her own mother had married young and that they'd lived on a farm, as the characters in her novel do. In speaking of the third and fourth novels, Martina concluded that a great deal of her writing derives from curiosity about her own parents, whose ages were very different, and that her fascination with the old Ireland comes from her love for her father, who was born in 1902. She also said that some people say all her novels are about the old Ireland, but she herself believes that the old Ireland still exists.

Martina's fourth novel has as its main subject that of Republican women. Her father fought against the British presence in Ireland in the 1920s, but they never spoke about it. There were things that couldn't be spoken of. Martina realised that she was trying, in her writing, to get a link back to her father's world. She said she was fascinated by Margaret Atwood's book, *Negotiating with the Dead*, where writing is seen as a journey to the underworld. Atwood argues that the dead actually want to speak, and call to the living to help them. She cited Derek Mahon's poem 'A Disused Shed in County Wexford', where the mushrooms have been waiting 'since civil war days', representing the suppressed voices of the people of that time, as evidence of what she meant. The silences were a question that Martina had to deal with: what did actually happen with her father? She knew that he and his friend had been captured by the Black and Tans, badly treated and then released. She also knew that the Black and Tans were themselves traumatised, dreg soldiers, the scum from other wars.

Suddenly she found that everything was leading back to her father. Her father would have seen men going off to the First World War, and heard them singing songs like 'The Boys from the Brigade', which Martina had thought was an IRA song, but later discovered was a song from the First World War. She felt that the need to enter her father's world was a strong urge throughout the book, even though she thought that she simply wanted to write about Republican women when she began. So the focus of the book changed during the course of her research. In researching her apparent theme, she discovered what she really wanted to write about.

In the early stages of preparation she was helped by a book called *My Fight for Irish Freedom* by Kathleen Clark, who was lady mayoress of Dublin after the war. Eileen Murphy, a character in the novel, is partly based on Kathleen Clark. After this, Martina spent some time working at the newspaper library in Colindale, north London. She told me that with the newspapers she had to let everything go in, absorb it, and then sit down to write without thinking about any of it at all.

A very early influence was her mother, who, she said, 'listens very hard and remembers a great deal, and had been telling me stories since I was a child'. (Martina is the tenth and youngest child in the family, so you can imagine how many stories she heard.) Martina's mother was born in 1919, and was herself picked up by the Black and Tans. Her grandma told her that they took her to a pub and spoke cockney to her, as if they were speaking French.

Martina discovered that the Black and Tans often picked up children, and that some of these children were Republican messengers, and were therefore in great danger. Some were killed by the soldiers. Tom Barry's book *Guerrilla Days in Ireland* told her more about the Black and Tans, about their uniforms and how terrifying they looked, and she gradually learnt about her father's part in this early, successful guerrilla war, which was led by young people, so the whole family had to get involved, and therefore the whole country.

After talking with Martina I realised that I needed to add an extra guideline to my checklist:

6. Be aware that your research might alter the focus of your writing, that during the course of your reading and thinking a character might step forward and demand your attention. Listen carefully for the dead who want to be heard, and let them speak through your writing.

Anita Lewton

Anita Lewton is a screenwriter and film producer. Her most recent production, in collaboration with Shane O'Sullivan, is a film called *Lemon Crush*, which is set in Chinatown and Soho, and is the story of a young Chinese waiter rekindling his friendship with his childhood sweetheart. This film has been screened at various international festivals, shown on Channel 4 and the Sundance Channel in the USA. Anita grew up in England and the Far East, and was a theatre director in the UK before moving to Los Angeles, where she studied filmmaking at University College of Los Angeles.

The film Anita is working on at present is based on an incident from her own experience, but with the characters and location changed. Her main character is a woman, a Scottish Italian in her thirties, who has the job of taking costumes for opera to Spoletto, a town in Italy. She is the single parent of a 12-year-old girl, although she leaves her child in Scotland while she travels. In Italy she makes contact with a younger man who is learning to be a webmaster and who wants to leave Italy. In the town, tourists come and go, and one of the film's themes is the human tendency to project the possibility of happiness on to another place, another person. The Italian man has a long-term girlfriend, but wants a way out of his present situation. The Scottish-Italian woman, like him, feels trapped, and there is the mood in the film of having no more chances. Balancing this theme of risk and desperation is that of duty: especially the woman's duty towards her daughter.

Anita told me that sometimes the setting of a film gets changed because of the possibility of development money. A film council will give money for a film based in one place but not in another. She said that this money can be crucial for a screenwriter, because the Media Plus programme in Brussels, for example, can give 6000 euros for a first draft. Obviously, this could keep writers going, and protect them from having to find other work while they are writing.

We talked about how themes might develop from film to film. When she was studying scriptwriting at UCLA, she managed apartments at Venice Beach to earn money, and worked in film studios at night. At film school, she noticed that her fellow students were tending to make coming-of-age films, with the theme of the father and the need to kick against his authority. In Anita's present film, one of the themes is the recognition, on the part of the woman, of her age. Anita said: 'When we grow older, we make patterns for our lives. My woman suddenly puts her head above the parapet.'

I asked her about how she found out enough to begin to write her screenplay. She described the process as 'like Ariadne with her thread', following the spool until she found what she wanted. For example: 'I had to go and see an Italian-American film. It wasn't very good, but I knew that I had to see it. I had to eat Italian food for a month. That was research, too.' She also spoke of the inspiration of her own life, her own experience: 'I've lived a lot as an immigrant. I was an illegal immigrant in America, and I feel like an immigrant here. My friends are from Ireland, Japan, New Zealand.' So the research is coming from within as well as from without.

Like Martina, Anita said that some research came from newspapers – stories about asylum seekers, for example. But she emphasised that you must do your research in your own way. Her co-producer, Shane O'Sullivan, researched a Senegalese character entirely on the net, and when his film appeared, Senegalese actors in Paris couldn't believe that he hadn't done the research work in the field. Another screenwriter, however, researching material on the education system in Jamaica in the 1950s, spent six months getting information from the Jamaican High Commission. There is no one way. You have to find your own methods of research.

From talking to Anita, I added two more points to the checklist, although you may have found more. Mine are:

7. Look inside yourself. The internal research will help you with what you want to write about.
8. Do your research in the way that is most comfortable for you. Use new technology if you wish, but use other resources too.

Jane Corbett

I then approached Jane Corbett, a novelist and screenwriter, whose latest films are *Chaos*, a TV film about a young man who teaches chaos theory at a university, whose wife is killed by a young woman stalker, and *Julie's Ghost*, which won the Sundance Award for the best independent film.

Jane echoed Martina's thoughts about the tendency of characters to change sex during the course of the writing. She said that in *Julie's Ghost*, the original focus of the film was the mother of Julie, who gets killed in a road accident. She knew that this focus wasn't right, but the story didn't seem to want to go away. And she said she often started a story with a young man, and then ended by seeing it from a woman's point of view. In *Julie's Ghost*, Jane wanted the main character to be an artist, and found that she became a textile designer, 'because a dress show is almost theatre, something you can show'. So here, the demands of the film medium, which requires something very visual, determined what kind of artist her main character would be.

In Jane's experience, you wait until the script is ready before you go after finance. She finds it takes about a year before a script is at the point where you can show it to producers. Jane works in close collaboration with the German film director Bettina Wilhelm, who does most of the research for the films. Jane tends to work by instinct, checking with Bettina ('How do we do this?') when she wants to make something happen in the film. The script editor Barry Devlin gave detailed comments on their present project, and Jane said she finds that a script gets better as different collaborators go over it and bring in different levels of meaning, implication and significance.

The script she has just completed is called *The Price of Miracles*. It's a thriller, but within a political context. Set in Johannesburg, it pursues an ecological theme, with pharmaceutical companies involved in drug experiments. At first, Jane thought that the setting of the film would be a European city, but she couldn't pinpoint, in her mind, which one. A sign, she said, that something wasn't right. Then one of the producers said: 'Why don't you set the whole thing in South Africa?' Johannesburg, with its frontier-town feeling, made sense to her, so, as in Anita Lewton's experience, the setting can end up being changed for all kinds of reasons. In the case of Jane's film, the setting changed to a place where there is the possibility of fewer checks on the drugs experiments that are taking place.

There is a trilogy of characters in *The Price Of Miracles*. One of the men was the main character at first, but then a woman of mixed race moved into the lead, someone with one foot in Britain and one in Africa, who only meets her father, a jazz musician, when she returns to Africa.

I came away from talking to Jane with two more points to add to the checklist:

9. You don't have to do all your own research. Friends and collaborators can help you. Ask them about what you need to find out.
10. Trusted colleagues can be invaluable when your script is in its early stages. Ask them to read it and give their comments.

Katherine Crawford

Katherine Crawford is a novelist and an art dealer. She has published a novel called *The Collecting Point* and her agent is at present trying to sell the film rights for it. Having read the novel, I agree that it's a particularly visual and exciting story, perfect material for a film.

Part of Katherine's life has been spent travelling in order to curate art exhibitions in different parts of the world. She told me that, sitting in restaurants on different continents on her own, the idea came to her of a young curator who decided to mount an exhibition of paintings that had been stolen, or bought for peanuts, by the Nazis before and during the Second World War. The story of how she achieves her ambition is the story of the novel.

During the action her heroine discovers how deep the collaboration with the Nazis went, that there are still many paintings of dubious provenance in state museums, and that the major auction houses continue to collude in the conspiracy of silence about who these art works originally belonged to. The novel looks at the prevalence of fraud in the art world, and one woman's struggle to make some sort of reparation.

The idea had been germinating in Katherine for a long time. It may have rooted in 1971, when she was offered a picture and asked if she would sell it by private treaty. This means that the seller either did not have, or did not want to show, the history of the painting's ownership. This was the opening in Katherine herself: the awareness that all was not well and that there was a significant snag in the fabric of her profession.

After this, she found that apparent accidents in her daily life were offering her more and more information which she could use in the novel. For example, a conversation at Los Alamos with a German friend told her a great deal about life in Germany during the war. Two terrible events in her own life – the illness and death of one of her sons, and then her own near-fatal illness – drove her on. She said that during the writing she was in a trance, thinking about what this or that character would do in a given situation. Katherine felt that she had to get the novel finished, no matter how many times she had to rewrite it. As an art curator, she had never felt confident about her writing. She knew that she had a good story, but she didn't know she could write it. By the time the novel was published and she'd read it to reading groups and been given much praise, she knew she could write. The novel therefore played a significant part in her own recovery.

Katherine did a great deal of her research in libraries. The Wiener Library in Devonshire Place, London gave her much Second World War material, and the archivists at the Royal Mint Library alerted her to the fact that a great deal of treasure and money was still hidden. When she encountered unhelpful officials, she sniffed further, did more research into the source of a painting and often uncovered fraudulent dealings and Nazi theft.

In 1997 there was a sale of looted art in Vienna, and a London auction house conducted a lecture on it, trying to absolve themselves from any responsibility or guilt. When Katherine asked who chose the artworks that were to be sold (implying that there may have been many that were not chosen to be sold, and therefore still in illegal hands), she was given no answer. The lecture fuelled her commitment to the project and made her recognise just how much treasure had been stolen and how much theft covered up.

After talking with Katherine I added two more points to the checklist:

11. If you can, work on a writing project that is interwoven with your own knowledge and experience. You already know about things that nobody else knows about. Use your own unique experience.
12. Trust accidents and chance conversations. Once you have your focus, the knowledge you need will come to you. Remember that the story wants to be written. You're just the conduit.

In my discussions with these five writers I became aware that there are many ways of doing your research. Everyone finds their own way, which may be partly dictated by the type of material you are investigating. So don't think that you have to follow a blueprint, because there isn't one. All I've done here is to distil certain guidelines from the experience of the writers, which I hope will be useful to you. If they aren't, you'll soon discover your own. Let me leave the last word with William Blake, rebel and visionary and peerless poet, who said: 'I must create a system of my own, or be the slave to another man's.'

14 Writing for yourself Alone

Creating a sense of self

We use writing for many things, not just for publication or to communicate with a wider public. Sometimes we write to make a problem clearer in our minds, to work out what we should do. Sometimes we write in order to save ourselves, to shore up some solid written thing in what might seem to be an ocean of chaos.

Anthony Storr in his book *Churchill's Black Dog*, which looks at the links between creativity and despair, explores the part writing can play as a means of creating an identity. Storr writes about Keats and Kafka, neither of whom believed they had a solid self to call upon. Keats's poems celebrate a merging with nature and with beautiful objects, although the poem 'Lamia' shows the fearsome side of this lack of fixity; and Kafka's writing laments the lack of a solid core. His lament amounts to a prophecy of the victimisation and destruction which was to be visited on the Jews soon after Kafka's death, and a prophecy, too, of the helplessness and fury many of us experience when faced with bureaucracy, or rule by officialdom.

It appears to me, from my reading, teaching and correspondence with other writers, that we can use writing as a way of creating an identity that might not yet exist because of our early experience of being neglected, abandoned or subjected to the whims of adults. Storr uses Charles Rycroft's definition of identity as 'the sense of one's continuous being as an entity distinguishable from all others', and Jung's description of personality as

> the supreme realization of the innate idiosyncrasy of a living being. It is an act of high courage flung in the face of life, the absolute affirmation of all that constitutes the individual.

There is a question that keeps returning to me in my own writing and in workshops with other writers: can the act of writing play a part in creating an identity for those who, for whatever reason, experience a sense of being incomplete, unrealised, half the person they believe they really are?

The ivory tower

Anthony Storr describes how this sense of being incomplete and isolated can come about:

> If guilt is boundless, if nothing the child does is ever right, he cannot develop any confidence in himself as an authentic person with a separate identity ... It is not surprising that people whose childhood experience was like that of Kafka tend to withdraw into an ivory tower of isolation where interaction with others cannot threaten them.
>
> *Churchill's Black Dog*, p. 65

In writing workshops we can use writing as another place where private thoughts can be set down. We can construct a bridge between our own private place and the place of other writers as we hear one another's work. Rapunzel lets fall her hair from the ivory tower of isolation and the prince enters the scene. The tower is penetrated by the presence of others who have made a foray from their own towers in order to hear and speak to the person who has just spoken from her own fortress. This is the efficacy of writing, that it is both profoundly inward and pressingly public: the most secreted diary seems to pulsate with a desire to be read, to be known. We speak with Sappho, with Shakespeare, both of whom are present to us despite their bodily disappearance.

Writing allows a retreat into the most private world, then tempts us out to want to speak with others. It allows us to converse with our illustrious ancestors, an activity that in our culture might otherwise be considered insane. Thus, it rescues an important aspect of primitive culture for our own benefit. It reconnects us with other identities, different from our own, who are nevertheless not trying to invade or overwhelm us. We converse with them over time in a way that does not destroy our *otium* (leisure). We are in our own tower, but looking outwards, rather than down on street level, *negotiating* (that is, negating our leisure. I owe this insight to Dr Dudley Young's fine book, *Origins of the Sacred*). As Anthony Storr writes of Kafka, 'writing was not only a way of affirming his identity without direct involvement, but also a form of abreaction, of laying ghosts by confronting them and pinning them down in words' (*Churchill's Black Dog*, p. 77).

One of the reasons we may need to write to shore up or build a sense of self is a feeling of impotence, of having no worth in the world or impact upon it. In 1952 the writer Dame Rebecca West made a radio broadcast. She described a visit to her godmother when she and her pretty sister Winifred were by turns ignored and insulted by a woman who was giving her mother an allowance, a woman she visited expecting to enjoy and admire. The broadcast said a great deal about social snobbery and the importance the godmother ascribed to refraining from relations of friendliness with those she believed to be socially inferior. But its chief interest for me lay in Dame Rebecca's description of what happened when her godmother turned away from her at a railway station. She spoke of the stiff, turned back of the woman who felt no need to say goodbye to someone who was beneath her, of her own tears of grief and rage at being so treated – and then the way her mind 'slid out to her godmother' in the cool, interested way a writer's mind will, in an attempt to understand the complex motivations of a woman who was both concerned for her family's welfare – she gave them an allowance at some cost to her own comfort – and equally concerned to make Rebecca and her sister feel small. It is this attempt to understand through writing, rather than to confront, challenge, lash out or turn the anger back upon oneself, that I find so fascinating. Rebecca West moves through her own experience of impotence and frustration into an attempt to grasp the whole scene: to comprehend through writing, rather than immediately to act, with the unspoken hope perhaps that this comprehending will enable intelligent action in the future.

There is a point in *The Communist Manifesto* where Marx makes fun of this endeavour. He says 'Philosophers have always wanted to understand the world. The point, however, is to change it.' But we know that we cannot change anything intelligently unless we have begun to understand it. Our own lives form a repeating cycle if we simply react to events without thought. It is my belief that the concentration of thought and energy that writing demands can lead to new modes of understanding, because we have begun to see our world in a new way, without fear. A Zen master, just before he died, instructed his disciples to 'Look directly. Do not be deceived. What is it?' When we have begun to look, the veil of illusions, presuppositions and prejudices that surround the object of our looking starts to fall away. We can see more clearly.

John Mortimer spoke of the way writing can convey a particular truth that other modes of discourse cannot because of the web of ritual we are caught up in with other people. He described a judge, dressed in red and carrying a nosegay, and claimed that the ceremony of entering the court in this way has less to do with life as most people understand it than a novel that is written about the legal profession.

In Cassandra's palace

Cassandra was endowed with the gift of prophecy by the god Apollo, who loved her, but when she refused to love him he changed the gift into a curse. She could still see into the future, but her punishment was that no one would believe her. Her prophecies were to be useless.

Cassandra could see clearly, but her knowledge could have no impact on the world. She is the archetype of knowing impotence, the woman who is shaken, inspired by foreknowledge but denied any power to avert disaster or enable a good outcome. She is isolated, scorned, taken away as a prize of war by Agamemnon, the man without compassion.

The act of writing can transform the impotence, the curse, back into a gift, if we can admit that a part of us is Cassandra, wailing, unheard, ignored, misunderstood; if we can learn to overcome the curse of the envious Apollo and allow our strengths to make sense again.

Apollo is an archetype, a presence in the psyche that we need to understand. Although he is intimately connected with art, poetry and song, he is also a god of order, of social bonds and boundary lines. He is not amused if order is changed or the bounds transgressed. He keeps the sun on its course and he wants things in their proper place, which is where he thinks they should be. When the satyr Marsyas picked up and played the pipe that Athene had made and then tossed aside, Apollo was so overcome with righteous fury that he had Marsyas flayed alive. His skin was torn from his body for making music when he was only a satyr, one of the lower orders, less than human.

I believe there is an Apollo in all of us: a nit-picking, smug, high and mighty part that does not like anything new to happen, wants to keep Marsyas as a beast-creature and Cassandra spouting impotent gibberish that no one wants to hear. We need to make contact with the Cassandra and the Marsyas within if we are to integrate all the notes of our writing voice: the low tones of rage and revolt and the high hysterical shrieking that cries out in the night and is never heard.

But this might feel like a dangerous step to take. Anthony Storr says 'It is surely the notion of *inspiration* which has been most closely linked with, and is responsible for, the idea that creative people are unstable.' To inspire means literally to breathe in. I am saying that if we allow ourselves to breathe in Cassandra and Marsyas, we will rock our own psychic boat, perhaps put ourselves at some risk as the neat god of order is threatened, but the strengths that Apollo has denied will begin to surface and enrich our lives.

We can make this risky transgressional move more effectively if we substitute *conspiracy* for *inspiration*. To conspire means to breathe together, and where two or three gather together to draw on the creative forces around an agreed-upon subject, the lines of communication between the ego and the deeper layers of the psyche can be held open: to break the bounds of convention, cliché and common usage and enable something new to be said.

Freud writes about primary and secondary processes in the psyche, and these are connected with the Marsyas/Apollo dichotomy, because the primary processes are concerned with the pleasure principle (crudely: things as we wish them to be) and the secondary processes are concerned with the reality principle (things as they are). But the two processes find a measure of connection in the act of writing. We combine together inspiration and rational thought, and when we conspire with others, reading out our own work and hearing theirs, then our own layers of thought are laid against theirs, providing a further opportunity to keep our inner and outer worlds connected. In one writing group, a writer asked if we could write about 'What is normal?' It seemed that Apollo was so strong in him that he found it hard to allow himself to do anything at all, in or out of the writing. He was perplexed about whether singing or talking or laughing to himself were within the spectrum of normal behaviour. Others in the group were able to reassure him, and he came up with a working practice for doing these things: 'It is normal as long as I can stop myself when I want to.' With a little help from his friends he had managed to put Apollo in his place, so he could not silence, before they had even begun, those conversations with the self that writers so much need.

Anthony Storr admits that there are risks involved when we begin to make contact with the creative forces inside:

> It has been demonstrated that creative people exhibit more neurotic traits than the average person, but are also better equipped to deal with their neurotic problems. It has also been shown that some of the psychological characteristics which are inherited as part of the predisposition to schizophrenia are divergent, loosely associative styles of thinking which, when normal, are 'creative', but which, when out of control, are transformed into the 'thought disorder' typical of schizophrenia.
>
> *Churchills' Black Dog*, p. 264

This is true. If we believe that the metaphors we use are literally true, then we need to consult the doctor. But if we can safely allow ourselves to describe a girlfriend's ear as 'a lightbulb ... South America' as one writer did in a recent group, then we are engaging in the risk-taking thought that produces good writing, the kind that pricks the hair on the back of the neck.

But we have to be brave enough to take the risk of seeing a lightbulb or South America in our girlfriend's ear, to transgress the boundaries of literalness and begin to stretch the meaning of words. *We have to be prepared to change the meaning of things.* And how do we do this without a solid sense of self?

I think there is a dialectical process at work. We often begin to write out of frustration or despair or a desire for some kind of revenge, and then the healing power of words comes subtly into play. Like Rebecca West, we move from rage and humiliation into a desire to create another world. Like John Mortimer, we respond to a deeply human need to create a world that is more real than the world we live in, with its prohibitions, bans and constrictions. I want to emphasise this element of healing, of drawing contradictory parts of the self together. As Anthony Storr says: 'The creative act is essentially integrative. Opposites are united; disparate elements are reconciled.'

Through the fear

If the self is divided, craving union with itself through the creative act, so, paradoxically, is the writer's material, language itself. Because language is divided into subjects and objects, things that do and things that are done to, active and passive, hammer and nail. Jill Purse, in her book *The Mystic Spiral*, writes: 'The distance between subject and object is knowledge; hence, in Japanese, the word meaning 'to understand' (*wakaru*) literally means 'to be divided'.

In terms of our own experience, to be divided against ourselves, to be unintegrated, involves a depletion of the energy in our minds and bodies. As the Bible says, the house divided against itself cannot stand. Yet again the dialectical process, where opposites are conjoined to form a higher synthesis, is at work: because when we explore our understanding, our divisions, through the system of supreme duality known as language, we can begin to remember ourselves as undivided and remember the face we had 'before the world was made'. For Yeats, who wrote this line, it is the lover who remembers the face of the beloved, and perhaps the necessary activity of the lover – mirroring and reflecting back with love and acceptance the beloved's face, mind and body – needs to be part of our exploration, our task of healing our own breaks, splinterings and dismemberments. We need to love ourselves without illusions, which is why our understanding is so important, to avoid falling for ourselves in the self-destructive way of Narcissus.

Writing is perhaps the only art that occupies this paradoxical position. Painting, sculpture, music and dance draw on natural materials, touchable things-in-themselves, that appeal directly to our feelings and our sense of beauty. Language, on the other hand, is abstract. It is nothing in itself – a word is here and then gone, it occupies no physical space in the world, and yet a few words can *make our day*, can change the meaning of the time we are living through.

Our language is made of subjects at work upon objects. It is a system where distinctions and discriminations are made at every point. If we were to try to describe *wholeness* we would be at some pains, because we would describe it in terms of its parts, its attributes or aspects, which would amount to breaking it down again, attacking it. Words by their very nature would break down wholeness into fragments, into *doer* and *done-to*. And yet it is through this system of divisions that we seek to mend the self and make it stronger. If wholeness is signified by silence, by the end of the need for words, then language signifies the search for wholeness. As Estragon says in Samuel Beckett's *Waiting for Godot*: 'In the meantime let us try and converse calmly, since we are incapable of keeping silent.'

We use words all through our lives, but in death we are quiet. We might speculate, then, that language, and writing in particular, because of its supposed permanence, is something we use as a bulwark against our annihilation. In *Origins of the Sacred*, Dudley Young says: 'We know little about Minoan culture generally ... but it may be ... that the Minoans were not very scriptural. (I say this because of all the major cultures they seemed to have feared death the least, and writing is above all an answer to such fear)' (p. 298). Where does the fear come from?

The analyst Melanie Klein proposed that as newborn infants we all experience the most dramatic fantasies of persecuting or being persecuted by our mother, whether or not these fantasies have any basis in reality. Could it be that writing is especially important when these fantasies have not been held or contained by the mother, when our fear of annihilation remains strong?

I once ran a writing group in which a writer, a journalist, found that a great deal of the writing he had done over the last months had been thrown away by someone. He linked the 'letting go' of his writing with the letting go of dying. He said, 'I kept thinking *all is transient* but ... but ...'. He did not finish his sentence and we left it in silence. But I concluded that he had hoped that writing would provide a mainstay against the transience, and that this mainstay had been summarily removed by the person who had trashed it, reduced it to rubbish, rather than allowing it to remain as the transcendent words he had hoped it would be.

Another writer, for whom the persecutory fantasies had been turned in on himself, wrote:

> because writing provides an alternative to suicide, it helps me avoid that decisive action and, therefore, leaves open the possibility of recovery. Over a period, writing provides some record of the rhythms of depression (the lapses, recoveries, lapses ...) and thus some annotation of recoveries in the past, keeping hope alive. The writing 'tells a story'. If that story can have a happy ending it may be of some use to other people, and that is a reason for going on ... It provides me with some-

thing to do (Francis Bacon once said that painting 'helped to pass the time') ... and as someone who has always found writing a way of clarifying thought and feeling, it may have helped me to some understanding of my condition and thus have made it somewhat less frightening.

There is a lot in this to ponder, but I would like to concentrate on the usefulness of telling a story, and particularly of putting ourselves in the story.

Romancing

The aim of a story is to give pleasure. It may inform and enlighten us also, but we won't want to read it unless it holds us: pleases, makes us laugh or weep, or hypnotises us with its compelling horror. We have to want to read it, or it isn't a story, but just marks on a page. A story isn't a story until it's been read and taken in.

When we put ourselves in our own story, we go back into our own past, into a time that was painful or joyful, and we make something out of it. The past is therefore not lost or gone, but a living part of the present, something that can contribute to our understanding of the way things are now. I remember two dramatic moments when writers made this generous move. The first was a story about a little girl of about three, left in a rented room by her mother who was out cleaning. The writer gave every detail of the room: the shabby furnishings, the smells, the texture of the air, soiled and unkempt, and most of all an urgent sense of what it is like to be left alone. She gave us her sense of abandonment so that we could look at it and also at our own. And the second was a story about drowning by a woman who had been in a terrible boating accident on the River Thames. She gave us exactly what it feels like to hold your breath for as long as you can and then to give in, knowing you are going to die. She was able to write this back from the grave, as it were, because the top of the boat was then ripped off and she came to the surface.

Both these stories felt like enormous gifts to their listeners. We *were* this little girl left of necessity by her mother, and we were the young woman losing hold on her life in the Thames. But the writers were also able to make a gift to themselves in writing them. They took something terrible and shaped it into a story that people would want to hear. They brought something back.

But what if what we bring back is too painful for us to write, or for others to hear? There are parts of human experience that make words into beggars, unable to carry the load. What do we do then? We can remember that when we go back into the past we can *do with it what we like*. This is the freedom of the writer. No one is asking us to write, we do it for ourselves, so when we face impossibly raw parts of our lives we can change them. And changing the past means that we can reinvent the present.

Doris Lessing's novel *The Memoirs of a Survivor* has a character who steps through a wall in her flat back into the past. The present is unbearable: London has completely broken down, anyone who can leave has left, the air is so polluted it can hardly be breathed. When she steps back in time, she finds herself in a kind of marketplace where there are pieces of cloth lying about. She comes to know that in order to move forward in the present, to be able to act, she has to do something with these scraps of cloth. She begins to piece them together. The more she joins the cloth, the more free she is to make decisions when she moves back into the present.

I want you now to begin to discover whether this is true for you. We may think that we know our own past, but if we intervene in it and make it other than what it was, then we are taking an important step, we are playing with reality, modifying actual events with the power of our imagination.

Take an event from your own life that you found particularly painful, something that a part of you simply cannot accept. Roll it around in your mind. Muse on it, dream about it. How could it have happened differently? What else could you have said or done? Is there another interpretation of what happened that will make you see it in another way? Now write it, playfully. You can do what you like with it. Afterwards, put it away overnight, then reread it. What effect does your intervention in your own past have on you?

A passage to the unknown

I wonder whether these excursions into and reworkings of our own past can change our perceptions of our present-day lives? With some writers I think they can. For example, one woman, who had lived a large part of her adult life believing that her parents did not love her, tried writing a story in which it was clear that they did. Gradually her vision changed and she came to see that the story was right: they had loved her, but in a way she had not been able to take in. This was a painful as well as a joyful discovery because it meant that she could now begin to live as a human being who knew that she was loved.

But another writer, whose early life had been wholly bleak, both because she was growing up in Nazi Germany and had unbearably cruel parents, found that going back generated a new bout of terrible depression. She said she wished she had kept a diary in the past because it would have been 'like money in the bank'. I wonder if for this writer the practice of swapping stories would be useful, to help break the hold of her own past. She might 'give' another writer some event from her own life and let them do as they wish with it, and they might give her something of theirs. She would then have the freedom of entering someone else's past rather than her own, and experience the relief of living in another place, with a wholly different set of rules and allowances. Because the prison of our own self can be a terrible place: the hard, narrow bed of our own deprivations, the walls to which we have cried out our fears and longings, walls that did not answer, the lack of a loving presence outside the door. *We need a change.* If our own past is intransigent in its terrors, if there is nothing in it we can work with, then we can make a virtue out of our lack of identity and allow our writer-self to enter the life of another person, living or dead, and focus on another story, one that may seem far from our own. In the end we will make it our own, we cannot help it, but still it will help us to loose the tyranny of our own past and transform our own relationship to it. In letting go of ourself we can find ourself in a new way.

Moving on

There are times in our lives when everything seems to be moving inside us. The life we are living in the present is not enough, we can feel changes taking place inside our mind and our body. We long to know the future, because it is frightening to feel our known world slipping away, and yet we want it to go, to have done with it. Robert Lowell said that three times in our lives we lose everything and have to start again.

It is during these times of loss, change and development that writing can save our lives. I remember sitting in my kitchen high above London one winter with three friends. We were watching a total eclipse of the moon. As the sky darkened and that dull, bronzy glow surrounded the black circle that had been the moon, I said without thinking: 'I feel as though I don't fit in. I can't relax. There's nowhere where I can be myself.' A woman turned to me and said: 'How can you feel at ease when the whole cosmos is telling you to do something different?' I laughed – it was a rather dramatic statement – but I knew then that this was the beginning of a change in my life, one I could not stop from happening.

All I could do was to wait patiently. But I couldn't be patient. I was mad with desire and longing to know 'the outcome'. And I think I would have lost myself completely if I had not taken the time to write. The poems that came were a diary of the turmoil inside and outside. If I was a ship being wrecked in a storm then the poems were parts of myself that I managed to save. Each time I was thrown in the air or to the ground by the force that was shaking me, I would find myself writing – not to try to understand the experiences or analyse them away – but to keep a record of the changes in the only way I could, through metaphor, the transformative energy in words.

My little ship did go down. I left one country and went to live in another, only to find that I could not settle. I returned with a suitcase, no work and nowhere to live. I had some clothes, and under the clothes, the poems, my only salvage. And as I struggled to build a life, I kept going back to the poems, with their images of animals and angels, the parts of myself I had been forced to learn about, and I knew that, even if they meant nothing to others, they had truly saved my life, because in the poems I had made images of the risks I was taking, and so had honoured my journey and my need to make it in my own way.

Really, changes are happening inside us all the time, not always as destructive as the one I lived through, but sometimes much more so. If we can watch and listen and bear witness to these internal quakes and waves and downfalls, the weather inside us, then we give ourselves the chance to strengthen our identity for the next stage of life, *because the writing enables us to know what happened.* Telling someone in speech, I found, was no substitute, because they would cast their own light upon it, however carefully they tried to listen. I had to tell my own story, and then read and listen to it myself. To create my identity in my own words.

Which brings us back to the beginning of the chapter, and in a way to the beginning of the book, where we spoke about writing making us more human. And finally, we need to remember that the work is important, for ourselves, but not for ourselves alone:

> I thought how the poet is the first explorer beyond the frontiers of accepted knowledge of the human heart; by subtle use of imagery and sound and rhythm, he brings a first order into the wild forest of raw lived experience. To the blind drifted hours in which we simply live without knowing that we live, letting life flow over us in a kind of dream in which fact and illusion are hopelessly mixed, he can give form and name. And by giving this, surely he can give us power to live more effectively, through being aware that we live; and eventually, when the armies of organised knowledge have followed up the pioneer trails of the poets, wisdom can become a public possession; we begin to know something of the facts of our lives and so in part become able to control them instead of floundering helplessly in the dark.
>
> Marion Milner, *An Experiment in Leisure*, p. 133

That may be a shade hopeful, but we can go for it anyway. What do we have to lose?

15　Reaching an Audience

The writer occupies a split world. One part, the part that writes, that creates something new, requires a protected private space, a 'dark backward abysm' out of which daydreams can be called up in security. The other part, the part that needs to communicate, to reach an audience, knows that it is necessary to come out of that darkly private place, to present one's writing in public, to gauge the responses of a listening group.

A good way of starting to do this is to either join an already-existent writing class (you can find one by looking on the noticeboard in your local library, telephoning the local further, adult or higher education centre or contacting the nearest Workers' Educational Association) or, if there isn't one of these in your area, by forming your own writing group. This is your way of coming out of the closet as a writer.

There are various summer writing courses in Britain and America. They can last for anything between a weekend and three weeks and they involve journeying to a place (sometimes a large house has been rented for the time, sometimes a college) where you will eat, talk, be taught, sleep, *live* writing in a totally concentrated way for the length of the course. They are usually organised by well-established foundations (the Arvon Foundation for example) and they offer you the opportunity of working with and learning from well-known writers.

Avoid the impulse to sneer at writing courses. Many people cut themselves off from great sources of nourishment and direction because they imagine that writing cannot be taught, or if it can, that you can't learn about it in a group. That attitude is perhaps more prevalent in Britain than in America. Remember that many of our best writers now teach as well as write (perhaps to supplement the income they earn from royalties, but also because they simply want and like to) and that you can learn a great deal from the writers you admire. Sylvia Plath and

Anne Sexton both attended Robert Lowell's writing class, and Lowell himself camped on Allen Tate's lawn so he could be with him and learn what one experienced poet could teach a younger one.

Surveying the market

When you've reached the point where you *want* publication, where seeing your work in print is necessary to you in order to feel you've made a permanent communication – then you have to begin the work of looking at the market, seeing what is published and by whom.

Haunt your local libraries and bookshops. Scrutinise the fiction and poetry being published this year. Can you see a pattern emerging? Can you see the kinds of books a particular publisher tends to market? Use your notebook here. Take one publisher at a time and look at this year's list. What is each one interested in? Can you discern an editorial leaning or tendency in the work they accept? One might be interested in modernist writing and another in science fiction, for example.

Take a good look at the *Writers' and Artists' Yearbook*, which lists the publishers of all the books on the library shelves, plus some you may not have come across yet. There are some quite small publishers who are particularly open to new work. Find who they are, then ask your library to get some of their books for you. Remember that you are a businessperson now, thorough and tenacious, determined to discover the best possible outlets for your work. In the *Yearbook* you will also find a list of small magazines which publish poems, stories and (sometimes) parts of plays. It will not list them all because small magazines come and go, flourish for a while then 'die, that poetry may live', as Gertrude Stein said. Some of these will be on the periodical shelves at your library and others you might want to send off for. It is in the pages of these magazines that I think we can see most clearly how editorial policy, whether it is conscious or unconscious on the part of the editors, operates.

As you begin to send your work around to the various publications, keep a record of which stories and poems have gone where. Be prepared for many, many rejection slips. The American poet Marianne Moore said that she had sometimes to send a piece of work to forty different magazines before it was finally accepted. You may feel depressed when your work is returned to you, feel a failure, but magazine editors reject work for lots of different reasons, not all connected with the quality of the work. Perhaps they did not like what you were saying – it didn't fit in with the way they see their magazine. Perhaps the magazine is full for the next three issues and they don't want to commit themselves any further ahead. If you sent your work to a publisher and have not heard from them for two months, you should write to ask them whether or not they intend to publish it. Remember that many editors produce their magazine with little or no subsidy, so they are, in effect, doing the work for love. Bear this in mind when you feel impatient or impolite.

Competitions

Literary competitions abound now. Some are local, some national and their prizes range from £10 to £5000. If you decide to enter a competition, be sure to find out first who the judges are and read some of their work. Not to imitate it, of course, but to gauge whether any of them are likely to be interested in the kind of work you write. If you don't think they will be, you can enter the competition anyway but not waste any energy on hoping for an award.

If you have entered many competitions and never won a thing, this might not be because your work is poor. Remember that the main judges don't see the bulk of the entries because the competition organisers weed them out beforehand. In a sense, the competition is judged even before it is judged. Philip Larkin, in his book *Required Writing*, tells a peculiar story about judging a poetry competition where there were no love poems or nature poems. He asked the organisers 'Where are the love and nature poems?' and they replied 'Oh, we weeded them out'. So you might have entered a wonderful poem to that competition and Philip Larkin never got a chance to look at it.

I think competitions can be fun as long as you don't take them at all seriously. They are a lottery but they probably waste less of your money than gambling on horses, and, as vices go, will not wreck your health as smoking or alcohol will.

Getting a novel published

Once you have seen which publishers might be interested in your novel, you begin the long process of sending it to one after another.

Send it to one at a time and be prepared to wait a good while for a reply. Write to jog them along after three months. Again, do not be dismayed by rejections. The work of a new writer is always difficult to place. You have no reputation to encourage a publisher; they don't know what to expect. Liza Alther's bestselling novel *Kinflicks* was rejected at least fifty times before it found a home, but when it did it earned her enough money to enable her to devote herself full-time to writing.

If you are able to find a literary agent who will take on your work, the process of having it looked at by publishers will be speeded up for you. You will find a list of literary agents in the *Writers' and Artists' Yearbook*.

To approach agents, write, giving an outline of the novel, asking if they would be interested in reading it. If they say no, it might not be because they don't like the sound of it but because their lists are already full and they are unable to take on any more. Alternatively, they may say why they don't like it – bitter, but still useful. Once a literary agent has accepted your work, you stand a better chance of getting it published, although this is still not guaranteed. The agent will send it around to publishing houses where she or he will have contacts, so your work will be seen more quickly and with a more benevolent eye. If and when it is accepted, the agent will take 10 per cent commission on your royalties. Also, the *agent* will deal with the rejection slips, not you.

Self-publication

The publishing world is not always ready for new writers. André Gide self-published his first novel with disastrous results (he took most of the copies, unsold, to the shredders) and Anaïs Nin typeset, printed and sold *Winter of Artifice* herself. If she had not done so, her work might never have been discovered by American readers. The American publishing world was not ready for her but her readership was. At this moment, groups of people are getting together to publish their own work. They might have been refused by mainstream publishers or alternatively, and this is the more likely, they are making a positive choice to do it this way, since self-publication means that the writers can determine exactly what goes into their printed work.

A possible scenario for self-publishers is this: you have been meeting with other writers for some time. You enjoy each other's work. 'Perhaps we could make a performance?' one of you suggests. You hire a room above a pub or in a community centre and hand out invitations to all your friends. You advertise it in libraries, schools and local newspapers and find yourself reading to an audience of about 35. You have a lovely time. You make people laugh. You can tell they like it because they tell you so. 'Why don't you make a pamphlet of all this work? I would like to read it,' says someone. You like the idea. You want to find out how you can do it.

There are quicker ways and slower ways but they are all hefty consumers of time. Be prepared for this. Let us say, though, that you simply want to see the work in print. As long as it has a cover and is held together by staples, that's alright with you. So you type it on the computer. You arrange the material into the order you want and have it photocopied, preferably using a photocopier that does the collating for you. If you have to do the collating yourself, lay each separate page-pile next to each other around the room and go round picking up one page after the other, until you have the whole pamphlet together. This is much faster and more fun if a group of you do it together. You design a cover, back and front, and choose a title. Then you photocopy that. You staple it all together. And try to sell it. With luck, you might cover your costs but don't count on it. There are many mouldering, unsold pamphlets in people's lofts.

Whether or not this small-scale self-publication works in terms of sales is less important than the extraordinary experience it can provide: that of working hard with a few other writers at making something, putting something into print. The tasks themselves – typing, photocopying, collating, stapling – are not intrinsically interesting but doing them with others, who are eager for the same goal, is.

Unless you have a lot of money you will need to think about the price of all this: you will need to cost your enterprise. What is involved? List all your materials, every part of the process that will cost money and find out beforehand what the cost will be. How many pamphlets do you want to produce? How many can you realistically hope to sell? Will the local bookshops take them on a sale-or-return basis? Remember that booksellers take 33 per cent of your cover price as commission. Distribution is often the small publisher's main headache, so canvass your possible outlets beforehand.

The more ambitious you are for how the magazine is to look, the more time-consuming and expensive your enterprise becomes. You will be looking for a typesetter, help with layout, so the magazine is designed as eye-catchingly as possible, and a printer. If you publish more copies than you can hope to sell yourselves, you may need a distributor. Much planning and forethought is needed before you embark on such a large project. I recommend that you read Gail Chester's *Rolling Our Own*, which explores the work and achievements of women self-publishers. You should also make contact with the Federation of Worker Writers and Community Publishers.

Useful addresses

You can contact the Federation of Worker Writers at 61, Bloom Street, Manchester M1 3LY.

The Arts Council Poetry Library publishes lists of poetry magazines (which often also publish short stories), lists of poetry and short story competitions, bookshops which stock poetry magazines and part-time day and evening classes in creative writing. The address is: The Poetry Library, South Bank Centre, Royal Festival Hall, London SE1 8XX.

Your future

What will happen now? You have begun. Indeed, if you have followed through all the exercises in this book, you have done a substantial amount of work. How will you keep going? Will you be encouraged, or disappointed? It is my belief that any writer, who takes their work seriously, makes it a priority and does not give up, will eventually win a measure of recognition. But how do we not give up? If our work meets with rejection letters and silence on all sides, will we ourselves, in the end, be silenced?

Writer, if you are ever in danger of losing your tongue, read *Silences*. Tillie Olsen can warn you about all the ways it can possibly happen, and show, too, how the best writers have gone quiet in response to discouragement and lack of understanding. Once you know the ways of the enemy, silence, you will be better armed for fighting it. Make yourself a present of *Silences* and keep it by you as a reference book. It is as useful as a dictionary.

The other thing to remember is that when you are caught in that fearful quiet, that sense of the hopelessness of ever writing again, then *any* commission, any writing task set by another person, is a lifesaver. Writing (reviews, letters, short articles, jingles – it is almost immaterial) always improves your writing, always cajoles the writing voice into life again, when it had seemed dead. Don't refuse any writing work that comes your way, even though at first it might not seem to coincide with what you want to write. Writing feeds writing. The more you write, the more you have to write and the stronger your writing voice will become.

Further Reading – Some Useful Websites and Addresses

Useful resources

www.Poetrylibrary.org.uk

This is the main website of the Poetry Library in London. It will give you information about the services the library provides, including poetry events and readings.

www.Poetrymagazines.org

This is the site that poets should consult to discover the names and addresses of many poetry magazines in Britain. The Poetry Library has now digitised the poems in most of the major magazines, and is continuing to update, so you can get a good sense of the kind of work different magazines like and publish just from looking at this site. Do still send for copies of the magazines you are interested in, though. You need to hold the publication in your hands and look through it page by page to get a real idea of what it's like.

The National Association of Writers in Education

This organization supports writers and writing of all genres in all educational settings throughout the UK. Its website is: http://www.nawe.co.uk.
Some other poetry websites: Writing-world.com/poetry; Poetry.com/ Poetry.org; Daypoems.net.

Poetry Book Society

This is a resource for readers, writers, students and teachers of poetry. When you join, you get access to the latest books and the best titles of the last 50 years, and you can find full lists from all major publishers and independent presses on www.poetrybooks.co.uk. Address details: The Poetry Book Society, FREEPOST

PAM 6642, Book House, 45 East Hill, London SW18 2BR. Tel: +44 (0) 20 8870 8403. Email: infor@poetrybooks.co.uk. Website: www.poetrybooks.co.uk.

The Poetry School

Offers courses, poetry events and a critical service where experienced poets will give you one-to-one advice and feedback on your poems. Contact address: 1A Jewell Road, London E17 4QU. Tel: +44 (0) 208 223 0401.

The Poetry Society

Also offers a critical service, working with a team of professional poets 'to send you constructive advice, specific to your personal abilities'. Address: The Poetry Society, 22 Betterton Street, London WC2H 9BX. Tel: 020 7420 9880. Email: infor@poetrycociety.og.uk. Website: http://www.poetrysociety.org.uk.

Recommended reading

The Poetry Business by Peter Finch (Seren)

In this book, poet, bookseller, editor and publisher Peter Finch brings his knowledge and expertise to bear on the problems of developing your writing and getting published. He answers questions such as: Are writers' groups worth joining? Where are the biggest markets? Which are the best magazines and publishers? How are vanity publishers to be spotted? How should a book be promoted? and How do authors prepare for readings?

Recommended magazines

Acumen. A poetry journal that describes itself as 'for writers and readers alike', containing poems, reviews, articles, news and views. Dannie Abse said '*Acumen* mixes poems and prose by celebrated and new writers who have something to say and say it well.' You can obtain it by writing to the editor, Patricia Oxley, at 6 The Mount, Higher Furzeham, Brixham, Devon TQ5 8QY. The website is www.acumen-poetry.co.uk.

Ambit. A quarterly journal containing poems, stories and pictures, edited by Dr Martin Bax, a well-known children's doctor who edits *Ambit* in his spare time, with the help of Kate Pemberton, the assistant editor. Obtain a copy by writing to Ambit, 17 Priory Gardens, London N6 5QY. But visit their website first to find out the cost of single copies and subscriptions: ambitmagazine.co.uk.

Envoi. Poems and reviews. Editorial office: 44 Rudyard Road, Biddulph Moor, Stoke-on-Trent, ST8 7JN. The present editor is Roger Elkin and the competition secretary is David Bowen, whose address is: 17 Millcroft, Bishop's Stortford, Herts CM23 2BP.

Iota. A quarterly selection of contemporary poetry, edited by Bob Mee and Janet Murch of Ragged Raven Press, 1 Lodge Farm, Snitterfield, Stratford upon Avon, Warwickshire, CV37 0LR. Email: iotapoetry@aol.com. Website: www.iotapoetry.co.uk.

The Interpreter's House. Poems and short stories. Submissions to Merryn Williams, 10 Farrell Road, Wootton, Bedfordshire, MK43 9DU. Subscriptions (£10 for three issues in 2004) to 53 Rowley Furrows, Linslade, Bedfordshire LU7 2SH. Single copies £3 + 50p.

The London Magazine. A review of literature and the arts. Poems, features, stories and reviews. Editor: Sebastian Barker. Head Office: 32 Addison Grove, London W4 1ER. 6 issues per annum, £32 p.a. in 2004. Email: admin@thelondonmagazine.net.

Magma. A magazine of poetry and writing about poetry, published three times a year in summer, autumn and winter in full on paper and in selection on their website. They are looking for poems which give a direct sense of what it is to live today – 'honest about feelings, alert about the world, sometimes funny, always well crafted'. *Magma* is run by a small group rather than an individual, and the editorial responsibility rotates. It's wise, therefore, to contact their website to get current information. Website: www.magmapoetry.com. The editorial secretary is David Boll, and the address for contributions is 43 Keslake Road, London NW6 6DH. You can also submit by email to magmapoetry@aol.com. *Magma* is unusual in this. At present, most magazines don't welcome email submissions.

The Rialto. Poems, an editorial and some letters. Editor: Michael Mackmin. PO Box 309, Aylsham, Norwich, Norfolk NR11 6LN. Website: www.therialto.co.uk.

Staple. Poetry, short fiction, articles, reviews. Submissions can be sent to either editor: Ann Atkinson, Padley Rise, Nether Padley, Grindleford, Hope Valley, Derbyshire S32 2HE, or Elizabeth Barrett, 35 Carr Road, Walkley, Sheffield, South Yorkshire S6 2WY. Allow up to eight weeks for a response. Staple is published in March, July and November each year.

American magazines

Local university libraries often have American magazines. For listings, you can consult *The International Directory of Little Magazines and Small Presses* (Paradise, California: Dustbooks); *Directory of Poetry Publishers* (Paradise, California: Dustbooks); *Directory of Little Magazines* (Mount Kisco, New York: Moyer Bell). These publications are available for reference at the National Poetry Library, but when this book was published they hadn't yet digitised them. As with British magazines, remember to send the correct postage for return of manuscripts, and make your covering note short and to the point. The Poetry Library recommends Peter Finch's book *How To Publish Your Poetry* (Allison & Busby) as a good guide for the preparation of manuscripts.

The following American magazines are held in the Poetry Library collection, among others:

- *American Poetry Review*: 1704 Walnut Street, Philadelphia, PA
- *The Cream City Review*: PO Box 413, English Dept, Cutrin Hall, University of Wisconsin, Milwaukee, WI 53201
- *Cumberland Poetry Review*: PO Box 120128, Acklen Station Nashville, TN 37212
- *The Manhattan Review*: 440 Riverside Drive, NY 10027
- *Partisan Review*: 236 Bay State Road, Boston MA 02215
- *The Plum Review*:1654a Avon Place, NW Washington DC 20007
- *Poetry*: 60 West Walton Street, Chicago, IL 60610
- *Sulfur*: 210 Washenaw, Ypsilanti MI48197-2526
- *Tampa Review*: Box 19F, University of Tampa, FL 33606
- *Verse*: English Dept, College of William and Mary, Williamsburg, VA 23185

There are many American poetry magazines, so it would be wise to consult an American poetry website to help you begin to find your way around them.

Australian magazines

The only Australian literary magazine I have read regularly (with great pleasure) is *HEAT*. It is edited by Ivor Indyk, and contains essays, fiction and drama, poetry and art. Subscriptions and editorial enquiries should be sent to HEAT, PO Box 752, Artarmon NSW 1570 Australia. Its website is www.mypostbox.com/heat, and contributions should be sent to HEAT, School of Language and Media, University of Newcastle, Callaghan NSW 2308 Australia.

Index

abduction, 84
abstract nouns, 19
adjectives, 20, 25, 27, 28, 30
adventure, 82, 128
adverbs, 20, 25
Akhmatova, Anne, 9, 10
Allende, Isabel, 142
ambiguity, 15, 16
Ambit magazine, 139
anapaestic metre, 134
angle of vision, 23
Apollo, 99, 111, 164–5, 166
Aristotle, 77–81, 86
Athene, 164
Atwood, Margaret, 3, 13
Austen, Jane, 17, 18

Bacchae, The, 97
Bashō, 33–4
de Beauvoir, Simone, 1
Bennett, Alan, 60
Besford, Sonja, 115
Bettelheim, Bruno, 52
Bishop, Elizabeth, 114
Blake, William, 66–8, 71, 160
Bly, Robert, 98
Boyle, Kay, 39, 45
breathing, 131
Brecht, Bertolt, 2, 71
buddy movies, 85

Campbell, Joseph, 81–9
Carver, Raymond, 145–6
Cassandra, 165
Castaneda, Carlos, 5
change, 52–5
Chardin, Jean-Baptiste, 23
Chekov, Anton, 51, 53
cliché, 20, 165

climax, 78–9, 86
Colette, 5, 26–8
conflict, 43
Collett, Mike, 128
Conrad, Joseph, 4
conspiracy, 165
conversation, 142–3
Corbett, Jane, 157–8
Crawford, Katherine, 158–60

Dante, 142
daydreams, 94–5, 100–1
Demeter, 64, 86, 87
denouement, 80, 85
departure, 82, 84
description, 14–25, 26
development, 78
Dhuibhne, Eilis Ni, 126
dialect, 38
dialogue, 36–47
diary, 171–2
Dickens, Charles, 90–1
Dickinson, Emily, 18, 122, 124
Dionysius, 86, 97, 98, 99, 101, 107, 111
Doolittle, H., 92
Dorfman, Ariel, 85
Dove, Angela, 137
dreams, 82, 128
duality, 167
Duras, Marguerite, 72–3
Durrell, Lawrence, 1
dynamics, 135

Eliot, T. S., 33, 45, 48, 50, 114, 126
English sentence, the 30, 31, 167
epistolary novel, 95
Eurydice, 97
Evans, Martina, 133–44, 153–5
Ewart, Gavin, 111

fears, 61
feelings, 128
film scripts, 155–8
Fitzgerald, Scott, 127
Fowlers, H. W. & F. G., 24
Freud, Sigmund, 91, 94

gender and writing, 3
getting ready to write, 5
Gilgamesh, 85, 87, 88
Giorno, John, 109
Gittins, Chrissie, 112
Gittins, Diana, 102
Godfrey, Peter, 107
gossip, 109
Gothic horror, 60
Grace, Harriet, 151–3
Great Expectations, 90
Grimm's fairy tales, 52, 63–5
Griffiths, Trevor, 57

Hades, 97
haiku, 33, 109
healing, 76, 92, 131
Heaney, Seamus, 149–50
Hemingway, Ernest, 15, 32, 69, 71
Hendricks, Gay and Kathlyn, 146
Hermes, 97
hero/heroine, 81–9
Hey, Celia de la, 116
Homer, 129
Hopkins, Gerard Manley, 4
Hughes, Ted, 104
humour, 57–60, 65

impotence, 164
initiation, 78, 83, 86
inspiration, 165
irony, 49

James, Henry, 49, 90
James, William, 91
Jami, 147
Jane Eyre, 90, 123
jealousy, 72–5
journey, 80–9
Joyce, James, 41–2, 45, 85–6, 91
Jung, Carl Gustav, 161
junk, 92

Keats, John, 15
Klein, Melanie, 168

Larkin, Philip, 4
Lawrence, D. H., 36, 38, 44–5, 55, 126
Lessing, Doris, 168
Lewis, C. S., 142
Lewton, Anita, 155–7
London Magazine, The, 140
Lowell, Robert, 28–9, 171, 175
lyric poetry, 97

Mansfield, Katherine, 53, 54, 55
Márquez, Gabriel García, 93–4, 125
Marsyas, 164–5
Marx, Karl, 163
Maupassant, Guy de, 49–50
May, Tim, 108–9
Mayor, F. M., 90
McEwan, Ian, 46, 77–81
Melville, Hermann, 4
memory, 92
metaphor, 11, 12, 13, 68, 71, 73, 75, 125, 127, 128–34, 172
metre, 67, 113, 130
Milner, Marion, 173
Mnemosyne, 126
Montaigne, Michel de, 16, 51
Moore, Marianne, 175
Morrison, Toni, 142
Morrissey, 147
Mortimer, John, 164, 166
Muses, the, 98
myth, 76–89, 94, 143–4

Narcissus, 167, 179–80
narrative prose, 7, 48, 56, 66, 76, 90, 141, 161
naturalism, 43
Neruda, Pablo, 126–7
Nichols, Grace, 22
Nietzsche, 127
notebook, 9
nouns, 19, 20, 21
novel, 90–7

Oedipus, 97
Olsen, Tillie, 90, 93–4
opening, 77–8
opening the storehouse door, 6

Orpheus, 97
Ozick, Cynthia, 40, 45

performing your poems, 137
Persephone, 84, 85, 86, 87, 88
Pessoa, Fernando, 86
Piaget, Jean, 54
place, 14–25
Plath, Sylvia, 174
Plato, 143
pleasure principle, 165
Poe, Edgar Allan, 62–3, 65
Porter, Peter, 111
Postino, Il, 126
prophecy, 164
protest, 135
Proust, Marcel, 91
psychoanalysis, 91, 94, 114
Purse, Jill, 167

Qur'an, 147

realism, 43
reality principle, 165, 170
renga, 108–11
reparation, 79
research, 151–60
return, 83, 88
reworking, revising, 19, 170
rhythm (*see also* metre), 5, 69, 130, 135
Rich, Adrienne, 5, 8, 14, 24, 25, 92, 100,
    141
Ringrose, John, 101–3, 105–6, 108,
    112–13, 114, 118–19, 120
Rivers, Joan, 57
Robbe-Grillet, Alain, 73–5, 164
Rosetti, Christina, 11, 12
rubaiyat, 120–2
Rycroft, Charles, 160

Sappho, 97, 162
schizophrenia, 166
sense of self, 166, 167, 171, 172
senses, 10, 27, 68, 69
Sexton, Anne, 175
Shakespeare, William, 2, 16, 50, 111–12,
    142, 162
short story, 48–55
silence, 139, 168

simile, 11, 12, 125
Smedley Agnes, 7
Solzhenitsyn, Alexander, 7
spirit of place, 14–25
Stein, Gertrude, 175
Storr, Anthony, 161–3, 165, 166
style, 5
subject and object, 30
Sun, The, 125

taboo, 84
Tarantino, Quentin, 87
Tate, Allen, 175
Tennyson, Alfred Lord, 128
Thomas, Dylan, 114
timbre, 135
Townsend, Sue, 58–60
Traherne, Thomas, 11, 12
Trevor, William, 77–81
tune, 135
Turnbull, Colin, 143
turning point, 79

useful addresses, 181–4

verbs, 20, 21, 25, 31
verse, 32
villanelle, 113–17
visualisation, 26, 28
voice, 136

Walcott, Derek, 98
Walker, Alice, 22, 90, 95
Warne, Sandra, 17
websites, 181–4
West, Dame Rebecca, 163, 166
Wharton, Edith, 54
Wilde, Oscar, 146
wish list, 102–3
Wittig, Monique, 95
Woolf, Virginia, 2, 46, 91
wound, 81
writing with the whole self, 10

Yeats, W. B., 4, 92, 130, 132, 167
Young, Dudley, 163, 168

Zeldin, Theodore, 141
Zen, 164